SOUTHERN CLASSICS
5 WAYS

TASTE OF THE SOUTH®

hm|books

SOUTHERN CLASSICS

5 WAYS

hm | books

PRESIDENT/CCO Brian Hart Hoffman
VICE PRESIDENT/EDITORIAL Cindy Smith Cooper
DIRECTOR OF EDITORIAL OPERATIONS Brooke Michael Bell
GROUP CREATIVE DIRECTOR Deanna Rippy Gardner
ART DIRECTOR Cailyn Haynes

EDITORIAL

EDITOR Josh Miller
MANAGING EDITOR Betty Terry
FOOD EDITOR Anna Theoktisto
ASSISTANT EDITOR Mary-Kate Tucto
RECIPE EDITOR Fran Jensen
COPY EDITOR Emma Pitts
EDITORIAL ASSISTANT Hannah Jones
CREATIVE DIRECTOR/PHOTOGRAPHY Mac Jamieson
SENIOR PHOTOGRAPHERS John O'Hagan, Marcy Black Simpson
PHOTOGRAPHERS Jim Bathie, William Dickey, Stephanie Welbourne Steele
ASSISTANT PHOTOGRAPHER Caroline Smith
STYLISTS Sidney Bragiel, Mary Beth Jones, Beth K. Seeley
FOOD STYLISTS AND RECIPE DEVELOPERS Melissa Gray, Nancy Hughes, Kathleen Kanen, Janet Lambert, Vanessa Rocchio, Jade Sinacori, Anita Simpson Spain, Elizabeth Stringer
SENIOR DIGITAL IMAGING SPECIALIST Delisa McDaniel
DIGITAL IMAGING SPECIALIST Clark Densmore

hm
hoffmanmedia

CHAIRMAN OF THE BOARD/CEO Phyllis Hoffman DePiano
PRESIDENT/COO Eric W. Hoffman
PRESIDENT/CCO Brian Hart Hoffman
EXECUTIVE VICE PRESIDENT/CFO Mary P. Cummings
EXECUTIVE VICE PRESIDENT/OPERATIONS & MANUFACTURING Greg Baugh
VICE PRESIDENT/DIGITAL MEDIA Jon Adamson
VICE PRESIDENT/EDITORIAL Cindy Smith Cooper
VICE PRESIDENT/INTEGRATED MARKETING SOLUTIONS Ray Reed
VICE PRESIDENT/ADMINISTRATION Lynn Lee Terry

Hoffman Media
1900 International Park Drive, Suite 50
Birmingham, Alabama 35243
hoffmanmedia.com

ISBN # 978-1-940772-42-4
Printed in China

CONTENTS

5 WAYS WITH

INTRODUCTION

AT *TASTE OF THE SOUTH* MAGAZINE we know good Southern food. For the past 15 years, we've been sharing authentic recipes, celebrating the very best that the South has to offer. Thanks to the hardworking team in our test kitchen, we've tested and tasted more than 10,000 dishes over the years, each one more delicious than the next.

The recipes gracing the pages of this craving-inspired tome are more than just the comfort foods we all grew up with; they're also dishes inspired by those icons of the Southern culinary canon. Yes, there's an amazing Caramel Cake—but just wait til you taste the Caramel Cake Trifle. Of course there's creamed corn, but my goodness, the Creamed Corn Spoonbread Muffins! And it just gets better from there.

This book celebrates the Southern favorites you love, in all of their traditional glory. But the twists, the recipes inspired by their nostalgic flavors, these are the recipes that will bring you back to the kitchen again and again.

—*THE EDITORS*

5 WAYS <small>WITH</small>

TOMATO PIE

LAID DOWN IN A RAINBOW OF LAYERS, tomatoes bake up into one of the most delightful of the savory Southern pies. Whether you choose your favorite cast-iron skillet or a pie plate, it all starts with a crust. Storebought piecrust will work in a pinch, but it's hard to beat the flaky goodness of a homemade crust. The extra-sturdy texture comes in handy for cradling the swoon-inducing elixir of molten vine-ripe tomatoes, creamy mayonnaise, and melty cheese.

One commandment before you get started—salt those tomatoes! We love tomatoes for their juicy flavor, but all that extra water can make your pie turn out soggier than you'd like. But the solution is oh so simple. Just slice your tomatoes, sprinkle both sides with salt, and let them rest on paper towels for about half an hour, turning once. This draws out the extra moisture, ensuring a just-dry-enough pie that's full of rich tomato flavor.

And although it's impossibly tempting to slice that bubbling pie right after you pull it out of the oven, we counsel patience. Like a nice steak, tomato pie needs to sit and settle. If you can bear it, wait at least half an hour. Then give in to temptation, and serve yourself a slice of the best pie in the South.

CLASSIC TOMATO PIE

Fresh summer tomatoes and basil
add bright flavor to this savory pie.

—— MAKES 6 TO 8 SERVINGS ——

½ (14.1-ounce) package refrigerated piecrusts

2½ pounds assorted heirloom tomatoes, sliced ¼ inch thick and seeds removed

2 teaspoons kosher salt, divided

1 cup grated Gruyère cheese

1 cup shredded Monterey Jack cheese

¾ cup mayonnaise

1 large egg, lightly beaten

½ cup fresh basil, thinly sliced

1 tablespoon chopped fresh thyme

¼ teaspoon ground black pepper

1 cup chopped red onion

Garnish: fresh basil, chopped fresh thyme

Preheat oven to 425°. Press piecrust into bottom and up sides of a 10-inch cast-iron skillet. Fold edges under, and crimp as desired. Refrigerate for 30 minutes.

Place tomato slices on paper towels; sprinkle with 1 teaspoon salt. Let stand at room temperature for 30 minutes.

In a medium bowl, stir together cheeses, mayonnaise, egg, basil, thyme, pepper, and remaining 1 teaspoon salt. Sprinkle red onion over prepared crust; top with one-third of cheese mixture. Layer half of tomatoes in an overlapping pattern; top with one-third of cheese mixture. Repeat with remaining tomatoes and remaining cheese mixture.

Bake until cheese is golden brown and center is set, 40 to 45 minutes. Let cool completely before cutting. Serve at room temperature. Garnish with basil and thyme, if desired.

FOUR-CHEESE TOMATO PIES

Filled with fresh flavor, these single-serving
pies make a great summertime lunch.

─────────────── MAKES 6 TO 8 SERVINGS ───────────────

4   ounces goat cheese
4   ounces feta cheese
4   ounces cream cheese,
      softened
¼   cup sour cream
¼   cup buttermilk
2   large egg whites
1   large egg yolk
1   teaspoon lemon zest
½   teaspoon ground black
      pepper
¼   teaspoon ground red pepper
¼   cup chopped fresh basil
Toasted Cornbread Crusts
      (recipe follows)
1   pint heirloom tomatoes,
      thinly sliced and patted dry
¼   cup grated Parmesan cheese
Garnish: chopped fresh basil,
      ground black pepper

TOASTED CORNBREAD CRUSTS

3½   cups crumbled cornbread
3   tablespoons melted unsalted
      butter
2   tablespoons water
1   large egg white, beaten
½   cup ground Parmesan cheese

Preheat oven to 350°. In the work bowl of a food processor, pulse together goat cheese, feta, cream cheese, sour cream, and buttermilk until smooth, stopping to scrape sides of bowl. With processor running, add egg whites, egg yolk, zest, black pepper, and red pepper. Process for 30 seconds. Stir in basil.

Divide mixture among prepared Toasted Cornbread Crusts. Top with tomatoes and Parmesan.

Bake until set and lightly browned, 25 to 30 minutes. Garnish with basil and pepper, if desired.

FOR TOASTED CORNBREAD CRUSTS On a rimmed baking sheet, bake crumbled cornbread at 300° for 15 minutes. Transfer to a medium bowl; stir in melted butter, 2 tablespoons water, egg white, and Parmesan cheese until combined. Press into bottoms and up sides of 6 to 8 small oven-proof dishes; bake until set, 10 to 12 minutes.

HEIRLOOM TOMATO *and* GOAT CHEESE PIE

Creamy goat cheese, along with chives, tarragon,
and dill, add a delicious tartness to this tomato pie.

———— MAKES 1 (9-INCH) DEEP-DISH PIE ————

4 to 5 medium heirloom
    tomatoes
2   teaspoons salt, divided
1   cup all-purpose flour
¼   cup plain yellow
    cornmeal
1   teaspoon sugar
¼   cup cold unsalted
    butter, cubed
2   tablespoons water
1   large egg
6   ounces goat cheese,
    softened
4   ounces cream cheese,
    softened
1   tablespoon chopped
    fresh chives
1   tablespoon chopped
    fresh tarragon
1   tablespoon chopped
    fresh dill
1   tablespoon chopped
    fresh parsley
1   tablespoon honey
2   teaspoons balsamic
    vinegar
Garnish: chopped fresh dill,
    chopped fresh parsley

Slice tomatoes ¼ inch thick, and remove seeds. Place tomatoes in a single layer on paper towels. Sprinkle with 1 teaspoon salt; let stand for at least 20 minutes. Press with additional paper towels to remove excess moisture.

To the work bowl of a food processor, add flour, cornmeal, sugar, and remaining 1 teaspoon salt, pulsing to combine. Add cold butter, pulsing until mixture is crumbly. Add 2 tablespoons water and egg, pulsing to combine. Press mixture into bottom and up sides of a 9-inch deep-dish pie plate. Refrigerate for 10 minutes.

Preheat oven to 400°. Let piecrust stand at room temperature for 5 minutes.

Bake until lightly golden, 10 to 13 minutes. Let cool completely.

In a medium bowl, combine goat cheese, cream cheese, chives, tarragon, dill, and parsley. Spread goat cheese mixture into prepared crust. Arrange tomatoes in 2 layers on top of goat cheese mixture; reserve additional tomatoes for another use.

Bake until tomatoes and filling are warm throughout, 15 to 20 minutes. Let stand for at least 45 minutes. Just before serving, drizzle with honey and vinegar. Garnish with dill and parsley, if desired.

GREEN TOMATO CORN PIE

Of course, when we say "green tomato," we mean tomatoes of the red variety that have not ripened yet.

—————————— MAKES 1 (9-INCH) PIE ——————————

3 to 4 medium green (unripe) tomatoes
½ teaspoon salt
1 tablespoon unsalted butter
½ cup fresh corn kernels
¼ cup chopped yellow onion
2 cups shredded Monterey Jack cheese
1 cup mayonnaise
1 teaspoon seasoned salt
½ teaspoon hot sauce
½ (14.1-ounce) package refrigerated piecrusts

Preheat oven to 350°.

Slice tomatoes ¼ inch thick, and remove seeds. Place tomatoes in a single layer on paper towels. Sprinkle with salt; let stand for at least 20 minutes. Press with additional paper towels to remove excess moisture.

In a medium nonstick skillet, melt butter over medium-high heat. Add corn and onion; cook, stirring frequently, until corn begins to brown, 3 to 4 minutes. Set aside.

In a medium bowl, combine cheese, mayonnaise, seasoned salt, and hot sauce. Add corn mixture to cheese mixture, stirring to combine.

On a lightly floured surface, unroll piecrust. Roll into an 11-inch circle. Transfer to a 9-inch pie plate, pressing into bottom and up sides. Fold edges under, and crimp as desired.

Layer half of tomato slices in piecrust; spread cheese mixture over tomatoes, covering completely. Top with remaining tomatoes.

Bake until crust is golden brown, about 30 minutes. Let cool completely on a wire rack before serving.

TOMATO PIE IN BLACK PEPPER CRUST

A black pepper crust gives this version of tomato pie an extra kick.

──────── MAKES 1 (9-INCH) PIE ────────

1½ pounds large sun-ripened
tomatoes, preferably yellow
½ teaspoon kosher salt,
plus more to taste
¾ cup grated Gruyère cheese
½ cup mayonnaise
2 tablespoons finely chopped
green onion
Zest of 1 lemon
1 tablespoon fresh lemon juice
¼ teaspoon celery seed
¼ teaspoon ground black pepper
½ recipe Black Pepper Piecrust
(recipe follows)
3 tablespoons chopped fresh basil
½ cup coarse saltine cracker
crumbs
½ cup grated Parmesan cheese
1 tablespoon unsalted butter,
melted

BLACK PEPPER PIECRUST

Makes 2 (9-inch) piecrusts

3 cups all-purpose flour
2 teaspoons kosher salt
2 teaspoons ground black pepper
2 teaspoons sugar
½ cup cold unsalted butter,
cubed
¼ cup cold lard or all-vegetable
shortening, cubed
1 large egg
2 to 4 tablespoons ice water
1 tablespoon distilled white
vinegar

Preheat oven to 350°. Slice tomatoes ¼ inch thick, and remove seeds. Place tomatoes in a single layer on paper towels. Sprinkle with salt; let stand for 20 minutes. Press with additional paper towels to remove excess moisture. In a medium bowl, combine Gruyère, mayonnaise, green onion, lemon zest and juice, celery seed, and pepper. Season to taste with salt. Arrange half of tomatoes in bottom of prepared Black Pepper Piecrust. Spread cheese mixture over tomatoes, and top with basil. Arrange remaining tomatoes over basil. In a small bowl, combine cracker crumbs, Parmesan, and melted butter. Sprinkle over tomatoes. Bake until top is browned, about 30 minutes. Let cool completely on a wire rack before serving. Set aside.

FOR BLACK PEPPER PIECRUST To the work bowl of a food processor, add flour, salt, pepper, and sugar; pulse to combine. Add butter and lard, and pulse until mixture is crumbly. In a small bowl, whisk together egg, 2 tablespoons ice water, and vinegar. With processor running, add egg mixture in a slow, steady stream until a dough forms. (If dough doesn't hold together, add more ice water, 1 tablespoon at a time, pulsing just until incorporated.) Divide dough in half, and shape each half into a disk. Wrap tightly in plastic wrap. Refrigerate for at least 30 minutes or up to 3 days. On a lightly floured surface, roll 1 disk of dough into an 11-inch circle. Transfer to a 9-inch pie plate, pressing into bottom and up sides. Fold edges under, and crimp as desired. Cover with plastic wrap, and refrigerate for at least 30 minutes or up to 1 day.

Preheat oven to 400°. Prick dough with a fork. Top with a piece of parchment paper, letting ends extend over edges of plate. Add pie weights. Bake for 10 minutes. Carefully remove paper and weights. Bake until crust is light golden brown, about 12 minutes more. Let cool completely on a wire rack. Reserve remaining disk of dough for another use.

5 WAYS WITH

PEACH COBBLER

WHEN IT'S SUMMER IN THE SOUTH, peach cobbler is king. Few things are more Southern than a peach—the stone fruit harbinger of hot days. Come summertime, many a practiced hand takes a paring knife to the fuzzy exterior of a juicy peach, deftly pulling the skin away from the soft flesh. (This is best done over the kitchen sink to catch the juice running down your elbows.) The only thing better than the simple joy of eating a ripe summer peach is transforming them into what is arguably the best of all cobblers.

If you grew up in the South, you know cobbler. Bubbling and sweet, this humble dessert can be made with any fruit that's ripe enough to pick, but peaches take it to a transcendant level. Mixed with sugar and spices, the golden fruit stews in its own juices under a golden, buttery crust. While it crisps up golden brown, the bottom soaks up just enough of that syrupy goodness to create a dessert that yields easily to the business end of a determined spoon.

Variations on this blissful summer treat abound, from versions bedecked with sweet biscuits to others crowned with a cake-like batter. But no matter how you prepare it, nothing tops this sweet and comforting dish. Well, nothing except a few scoops of your favorite ice cream.

CLASSIC PEACH COBBLER

Sweet summer peaches bubble underneath
this buttery, stir-together crust.

─── MAKES ABOUT 8 SERVINGS ───

½ cup unsalted butter
1 cup all-purpose flour
1 cup sugar
1 tablespoon baking powder
1 cup whole buttermilk
1 cup firmly packed light brown sugar
1½ tablespoons cornstarch
½ teaspoon ground cinnamon
½ teaspoon kosher salt
¼ teaspoon ground nutmeg
5 cups peeled, pitted, and sliced fresh peaches
1 tablespoon vanilla extract
Vanilla ice cream, to serve

Preheat oven to 375°. In a 2-quart baking dish, place butter. Place dish in oven to melt butter, about 5 minutes.

In another bowl, combine flour, sugar, and baking powder. Add buttermilk, whisking until smooth. Pour buttermilk mixture over melted butter in baking dish; do not stir. Set aside.

In a medium saucepan, whisk together brown sugar, cornstarch, cinnamon, salt, and nutmeg. Add peaches and vanilla, stirring to combine. Cook over medium-high heat, stirring often, until mixture boils; remove from heat. Pour peach mixture over batter.

Bake until peaches are bubbly and crust is golden brown, about 45 minutes. Remove from oven, and let cool slightly. Serve warm with vanilla ice cream, if desired.

PEACH-BLUEBERRY COBBLER

*Fresh peaches and blueberries melt together
beneath a layer of buttery crumble.*

─── **MAKES ABOUT 8 SERVINGS** ───

6 to 8 cups peeled, pitted, and
    sliced fresh peaches (about
    8 medium peaches)
1½ cups fresh blueberries
¼   cup bourbon
⅔   cup plus 1 teaspoon
    sugar, divided
2½ tablespoons cornstarch
1   teaspoon ground cinnamon
¾   cup all-purpose flour
1   teaspoon baking powder
¼   teaspoon salt
6   tablespoons cold unsalted
    butter, cubed
½   cup heavy whipping cream
Vanilla ice cream, to serve

Preheat oven to 375°.

In a medium bowl, combine peaches, blueberries, bourbon, ⅓ cup sugar, cornstarch, and cinnamon.

In another medium bowl, whisk together flour, ⅓ cup sugar, baking powder, and salt. Using a pastry blender or 2 forks, cut in butter until mixture is crumbly. Add cream, stirring gently just until dough forms. Spoon fruit mixture into a 10-inch cast-iron skillet; top with crumbled dough. Sprinkle with remaining 1 teaspoon sugar.

Bake until top is golden brown and filling is bubbly, about 45 minutes. Serve with ice cream, if desired.

3

PEACH COBBLER ICE CREAM

Filled with crumbled sweet biscuits and ripe peaches,
this ice cream is the perfect summer treat.

—————————— MAKES ABOUT 1 GALLON ——————————

Almond Shortbread Topping
    (recipe follows)
4   cups peeled, pitted, and
    chopped fresh peaches
½   cup sugar
1   tablespoon fresh orange
    juice
1   tablespoon bourbon
    (optional)
2   teaspoons cornstarch
3   tablespoons water
2   cups heavy whipping cream
2   (14-ounce) cans sweetened
    condensed milk
4   cups half-and-half
1   tablespoon almond extract

ALMOND SHORTBREAD TOPPING
1¼ cups all-purpose flour
½   cup sugar
1½ teaspoons baking powder
1   teaspoon kosher salt
6   tablespoons cold unsalted
    butter, cubed
½   cup heavy whipping cream
½   cup sliced almonds

Preheat oven to 350°. Line a rimmed baking sheet with parchment paper. Divide Almond Shortbread Topping into 8 rounds; place 1 inch apart on prepared pan. Bake until golden brown, 12 to 15 minutes. Let cool slightly; crumble.

In a large skillet, combine peaches, sugar, orange juice, and bourbon (if using) over medium heat. Cook for 8 to 10 minutes, stirring occasionally. In a small bowl, whisk together cornstarch and 3 tablespoons water; stir into peach mixture. Cook 2 minutes more, stirring frequently. Remove from heat.

In a large bowl, beat cream with a mixer at high speed until stiff peaks form, 4 to 6 minutes. Add condensed milk; beat until stiff peaks form, 2 to 3 minutes. Stir in half-and-half and almond extract.

Freeze in an ice cream maker according to manufacturer's instructions for 30 minutes. Stir in peach mixture and crumbled Almond Shortbread Topping. Freeze for 2 hours or overnight.

FOR ALMOND SHORTBREAD TOPPING In a large bowl, stir together flour, sugar, baking powder, and salt. Using a pastry blender or 2 forks, cut in cold butter until mixture is crumbly. Stir in cream and almonds just until combined. (Mixture will be crumbly.)

Using your hands, gently shape dough into a disk. Wrap in plastic wrap, and refrigerate until ready to use.

PEACH COBBLER BARS

These bars will help you get your cobbler fix on the go—no spoon required!

MAKES ABOUT 12 SERVINGS

2   cups firmly packed light brown sugar, divided
3   tablespoons cornstarch
½   teaspoon ground cinnamon
¼   teaspoon ground nutmeg
¼   teaspoon ground ginger
8   cups peeled, pitted, and diced fresh peaches (about 8 peaches)
1   tablespoon orange zest
2   tablespoons fresh orange juice
3   cups all-purpose flour
1   cup old-fashioned oats
1½ teaspoons baking powder
1   teaspoon salt
1   cup cold unsalted butter, cubed
1   large egg
½   cup sour cream
1½ teaspoons vanilla extract

Preheat oven to 350°. Line a 13x9-inch baking pan with foil; spray with baking spray with flour.

In a large bowl, stir together 1 cup brown sugar, cornstarch, cinnamon, nutmeg, and ginger. Stir in peaches and orange zest and juice until combined.

In another large bowl, whisk together flour, oats, baking powder, salt, and remaining 1 cup brown sugar. Using a pastry blender or 2 forks, cut in cold butter until mixture is crumbly. In a small bowl, whisk together egg, sour cream, and vanilla until smooth. Add egg mixture to flour mixture, stirring until combined.

Using a measuring cup, press three-fourths of flour mixture into bottom of prepared pan. Stir peach mixture; spread onto flour mixture in pan. Sprinkle with remaining flour mixture.

Bake until browned and set, 40 to 45 minutes.

5

PEACH-GINGER COBBLERS

Ginger adds a hint of warm spice to these sweet peach cobblers.

MAKES 6

½ cup unsalted butter, softened

¼ cup granulated sugar

¾ cup firmly packed light brown sugar, divided

1 cup plus 3 tablespoons all-purpose flour, divided

½ teaspoon ground nutmeg

¼ teaspoon ground ginger

¼ teaspoon kosher salt

6 to 8 cups peeled, pitted, and sliced fresh peaches (about 8 medium peaches)

1½ tablespoons grated fresh ginger

1 tablespoon fresh lemon juice

½ teaspoon vanilla extract

½ teaspoon ground cinnamon

1 large egg, lightly beaten

3 tablespoons turbinado sugar

Preheat oven to 375°. Spray 6 (4½-inch) cast-iron skillets with cooking spray.

In a large bowl, beat butter with a mixer at medium speed until creamy. Add granulated sugar and ¼ cup brown sugar; beat until fluffy.

In a medium bowl, combine 1 cup flour, nutmeg, ground ginger, and salt. Stir flour mixture into butter mixture in 2 batches. Shape dough into a disk. Wrap in plastic wrap, and refrigerate for at least 30 minutes.

In a large bowl, stir together peaches, grated ginger, lemon juice, vanilla, cinnamon, remaining ½ cup brown sugar, and remaining 3 tablespoons flour. Spoon peach mixture into prepared skillets. Place on a baking sheet, and bake for 15 minutes.

On a lightly floured surface, roll dough to ¼-inch thickness. Using a 3-inch round cutter dipped in flour, cut dough into 6 circles. Top each skillet with a circle. Brush dough with egg; sprinkle with turbinado sugar. Bake until tops are golden brown and filling is bubbly, about 30 minutes more.

5 WAYS WITH
CREAMED CORN

THERE'S JUST SOMETHING ABOUT CORN that seems magical. It can be ground into meal for cornbread, popped until light and crunchy, or simply grilled and eaten straight off the cob. But our favorite way to prepare this golden treasure of Southern vegetable gardens is creamed corn, by far. In leaner times, it was prepared with no cream at all—only a vigorous scraping of the bare cob to release the "milk" that gives the best creamed corn its delicious texture.

Of course, there's nothing wrong with adding a touch of cream and butter for a little extra richness. But whatever you do, start with freshly shucked ears of ripe summer corn. A sharp knife makes easy work of removing the kernels and raking down the sides of the cob to extract every bit of flavor.

Sweet, savory, and creamy all in one, with a slight crunch from the whole kernels, creamed corn is a bubbling skillet full of Southern comfort. A word to the wise—be sure to stir as it simmers to ward off any burnt bits in your pot of gold. And to keep every decadent spoonful warm, serve it family-style, straight from your favorite cast-iron skillet.

CLASSIC CREAMED CORN

Accented with the sweet flavor of Vidalia onions,
this creamed corn is heaven by the spoonful.

MAKES ABOUT 5 CUPS

18 medium ears fresh corn, shucked

3 tablespoons unsalted butter, plus more to serve

¾ cup chopped yellow onion

1½ teaspoons kosher salt, divided

¼ cup heavy whipping cream

1 tablespoon chopped fresh thyme

¼ teaspoon ground black pepper

⅛ teaspoon ground red pepper

Holding a long, sharp knife at a downward angle, cut tips from corn kernels (about 4 cups). Stand each cob over a large bowl. Using the back of a knife, scrape downward to remove pulp (about 3 cups).

In a 10-inch skillet, melt 3 tablespoons butter over medium heat. Add onion; cover and cook over medium-low heat until softened, about 15 minutes.

Add corn kernel tips, pulp, and 1 teaspoon salt; bring to a boil over medium-high heat. Cover, reduce heat, and simmer, stirring occasionally, until corn is tender, about 35 minutes.

Uncover; stir in cream, thyme, black pepper, red pepper, and remaining ½ teaspoon salt. Cook until thickened, 8 to 10 minutes. Serve with extra butter.

CREAMED CORN FRITTERS

Served with a sweet and spicy pepper jelly, these fritters are the perfect appetizer for any summer gathering.

───────── MAKES ABOUT 24 ─────────

¾ cup red pepper jelly
2 tablespoons water
1 tablespoon stone-ground mustard
Vegetable oil, for frying
1½ cups self-rising flour
¼ cup plain cornmeal
¼ cup grated Parmesan cheese
1 cup Classic Creamed Corn (recipe on page 37)
1 large egg
½ cup whole milk

In a small bowl, whisk together pepper jelly, 2 tablespoons water, and mustard. Set aside.

Fill a small Dutch oven halfway full with oil, and heat over medium-high heat until a deep-fry thermometer registers 350°.

In a large bowl, whisk together flour, cornmeal, and cheese. In a medium bowl, whisk together Classic Creamed Corn, egg, and milk. Make a well in center of dry ingredients. Add milk mixture, stirring just until moistened.

Working in batches, drop batter by tablespoonfuls into hot oil. Fry, turning occasionally, until golden brown, about 3 minutes. Remove using a slotted spoon, and let drain on paper towels. Serve with red pepper jelly mixture.

3

CREAMED CORN SPOONBREAD MUFFINS

Slathered with smoky bacon butter, these muffins are a knockout.

MAKES 12

BACON BUTTER

- 6 slices bacon
- 1 cup unsalted butter, softened
- ¼ teaspoon kosher salt

MUFFINS

- 1 cup all-purpose flour
- 1 cup plain stone-ground cornmeal
- 1 tablespoon baking powder
- 1½ teaspoons kosher salt
- 1¼ cups Classic Creamed Corn (recipe on page 37)
- ½ cup whole milk
- ½ cup unsalted butter, melted
- 1 large egg
- 2 large egg whites

FOR BACON BUTTER In a large skillet, cook bacon over medium heat until crisp. Remove bacon, and let drain on paper towels, reserving ¼ cup bacon drippings in a bowl. Let bacon cool completely; crumble.

In a medium bowl, stir together crumbled bacon, butter, and salt. Cover and refrigerate until ready to use.

Preheat oven to 425°. Pour 1 teaspoon reserved bacon drippings into 12 muffin cups. Place in oven until drippings are very hot, about 8 minutes.

FOR MUFFINS In a large bowl, whisk together flour, cornmeal, baking powder, and salt. In a medium bowl, whisk together Classic Creamed Corn, milk, melted butter, and egg. Make a well in center of dry ingredients. Add milk mixture, stirring just until moistened. In another medium bowl, beat egg whites with a mixer at high speed until stiff peaks form. Fold egg whites into batter. Carefully divide batter among prepared muffin cups.

Bake until a wooden pick inserted in center comes out clean, about 12 minutes. Let cool in pan for 5 minutes. Run a knife around edge of cups; remove muffins. Serve warm with bacon butter.

4

CREAMED CORN *AND* RICE-STUFFED BELL PEPPERS

Perfect for a meatless supper, these peppers taste just like enchiladas.

MAKES 8 SERVINGS
---

3   tablespoons unsalted butter
½   cup finely chopped yellow onion
1   cup long-grain rice
2   cloves garlic, minced
2   cups chicken broth
1¼ teaspoons kosher salt
2   cups Classic Creamed Corn (recipe on page 37)
1   cup shredded sharp Cheddar cheese, divided
1   cup shredded Monterey Jack cheese, divided
½   cup chopped fresh cilantro
½   teaspoon ground ancho chile powder
½   teaspoon ground cumin
4   medium red bell peppers
2   tablespoons water
1   tablespoon canola oil

In a large saucepan, melt butter over medium-high heat. Add onion; cook for 1 minute. Add rice and garlic; cook for 1 minute. Stir in broth and salt; bring to a boil. Reduce heat to medium-low. Cover and simmer until liquid is absorbed and rice is tender, about 15 minutes. Remove from heat. Gently stir in Classic Creamed Corn, ½ cup Cheddar, ½ cup Monterey Jack, cilantro, chile powder, and cumin.

Preheat oven to 350°. Cut bell peppers in half lengthwise, discarding seeds and membranes. Place peppers, cut side up, in a microwave-safe 13x9-inch baking dish. Add 2 tablespoons water to dish. Lightly cover with wax paper. Microwave until peppers begin to soften, about 3 minutes. Drain any excess liquid. Fill peppers, mounding rice mixture in each pepper half. Drizzle with oil. Cover with foil.

Bake until tender and heated through, about 35 minutes. Uncover; sprinkle with remaining ½ cup Cheddar and remaining ½ cup Monterey Jack. Bake until cheese is melted, about 10 minutes more.

SHRIMP *and* CREAMED CORN GRITS

*Boiling the husks and cobs adds rich corn flavor
to this spin on classic shrimp and grits.*

— MAKES 4 SERVINGS —

GRITS

5⅔	cups chicken broth
6	corn husks
2	corn cobs
1¼	cups stone-ground grits
1½	teaspoons kosher salt
¼	teaspoon ground black pepper
1	cup Classic Creamed Corn (recipe on page 37)
2	tablespoons unsalted butter
2	tablespoons heavy whipping cream

SHRIMP

4	tablespoons unsalted butter, divided
1	tablespoon canola oil
1½	pounds medium fresh shrimp, peeled and deveined (tails left on)
¾	teaspoon kosher salt
¼	teaspoon ground black pepper
1	tablespoon fresh lemon juice
1	teaspoon hot sauce
½	cup cherry tomatoes, quartered
½	cup torn fresh basil
⅓	cup chopped green onion
¼	cup chopped fresh parsley

FOR GRITS In a large saucepan, bring broth, corn husks, and corn cobs to a simmer over medium heat. Reduce heat to low; cover and cook for 30 minutes.

Discard husks and cobs. Reserve ⅔ cup broth. Bring remaining broth to a boil over medium-high heat. Whisk in grits, salt, and pepper until combined. Reduce heat to medium-low. Partially cover and simmer, stirring occasionally, until thickened and tender, about 40 minutes.

Remove from heat. Add Classic Creamed Corn, butter, and cream, stirring until butter is melted. Cover and set aside.

FOR SHRIMP In a large skillet, heat 2 tablespoons butter and oil over medium-high heat. Sprinkle shrimp with salt and pepper. Add half of shrimp to skillet; cook, turning occasionally, until pink and firm, about 3 minutes. Remove shrimp from skillet. Repeat with remaining shrimp. Add reserved ⅔ cup broth, lemon juice, and hot sauce to skillet, scraping browned bits from bottom of skillet with a wooden spoon. Reduce heat to low. Add remaining 2 tablespoons butter to skillet. Cook, stirring frequently, until butter is melted. Return shrimp to skillet, stirring well. Serve shrimp mixture with grits, tomatoes, basil, green onion, and parsley. Sprinkle with additional salt and pepper, if desired.

5 WAYS WITH

CATFISH

IF YOU GREW UP IN THE SOUTH, the first fish you remember eating is probably catfish. Dredged in cornmeal and fried to a golden crispness, it has been a mainstay at church fundraisers, family reunions, and neighborhood fish frys for generations.

Our bewhiskered friend has a long history in Southern foodways. Native Americans were enjoying catfish long before European colonists arrived on Southern shores. Catfish is commonly found in lakes and rivers throughout the region, and it's easy to catch. A good-sized catfish can be stretched to feed a whole family. A little cornmeal, a dash of cayenne pepper (both of which you'll find in any Southern pantry), and a cast-iron kettle of hot oil, and you've got yourself a fish fry.

Three Southern cities claim to be the catfish capital of the world—Belzoni, Mississippi; Savannah, Tennessee; and Des Allemands, Louisiana. Belzoni is a center for farm-raised catfish, while Savannah has built its reputation on wild-caught catfish from the Tennessee River. Not to be outdone, Des Allemands pulls its catfish from the bayous of the Atchafalaya River basin.

In the end, we'd have to agree with 19th century writer Mark Twain, who wrote, "The catfish is a plenty good enough fish for anybody."

CLASSIC FRIED CATFISH
WITH FRIED PICKLES

Since the oil's already hot, why not fry up a batch of pickles, too?

—————————— MAKES ABOUT 6 SERVINGS ——————————

2 cups whole buttermilk, divided
2 teaspoons hot pepper sauce, divided
3 cups plain cornmeal
1 cup all-purpose flour
1½ tablespoons kosher salt
1½ teaspoons garlic powder
1½ teaspoons paprika
1 (24-ounce) jar bread-and-butter pickle slices, drained
Vegetable oil, for frying
6 (6-ounce) catfish fillets
Lemon wedges

In a medium bowl, combine 1 cup buttermilk and 1 teaspoon hot pepper sauce. In a large shallow dish, whisk together cornmeal, flour, salt, garlic powder, and paprika. Working in batches, dip pickle slices in buttermilk mixture, letting excess drip off. Dredge in cornmeal mixture, shaking off excess. Discard buttermilk mixture; reserve remaining cornmeal mixture.

In a large cast-iron skillet, pour oil to a depth of 2 inches, and heat over medium heat until a deep-fry thermometer registers 350°. Fry pickles in batches, turning occasionally, until golden brown, about 2 minutes. Remove with a slotted spoon, and let drain on paper towels.

In a medium bowl, combine remaining 1 cup buttermilk and remaining 1 teaspoon hot pepper sauce. Working in batches, dip fish in buttermilk mixture, letting excess drip off. Dredge in cornmeal mixture, shaking off excess. Fry, turning occasionally, until golden brown, about 4 minutes. Let drain on paper towels. Serve with fried pickles and lemon wedges.

GRILLED CATFISH with ONION-POBLANO RELISH

Mojo marinade lends Latin flavor to these tender catfish fillets.

— MAKES 4 SERVINGS —

4   (6-ounce) catfish fillets
1   cup mojo marinade*
3   tablespoons vegetable oil,
     divided
½   teaspoon kosher salt
¼   teaspoon ground black
     pepper
Onion-Poblano Relish
     (recipe follows)
Garnish: thinly sliced radishes

We used Goya Mojo Criollo Marinade.

ONION-POBLANO RELISH
2   medium poblano peppers
1   medium Vidalia or sweet
     onion, cut into wedges
2   tablespoons vegetable oil,
     divided
½   cup chopped fresh cilantro
¼   cup chopped green onion
1   tablespoon fresh lime juice
¼   teaspoon kosher salt
¼   teaspoon crushed red pepper
⅛   teaspoon ground cumin
⅛   teaspoon garlic powder

In a large shallow dish, combine fish and marinade; cover and refrigerate for 30 minutes.

Remove fish from marinade; discard marinade. Pat fish dry with paper towels. Brush with 2 tablespoons oil, and sprinkle with salt and pepper.

Brush a cast-iron grill pan with remaining 1 tablespoon oil, and heat over medium-high heat. Add fish, and cook until fish can be easily turned with a spatula, about 3 minutes. Turn fish; cook until fish is opaque and flakes easily with a fork, about 2 minutes more. Serve with Onion-Poblano Relish. Garnish with radish slices, if desired.

FOR ONION-POBLANO RELISH Cut poblano peppers in half lengthwise; discard seeds. Flatten peppers. Brush peppers and onion wedges with 1 tablespoon oil.

Brush a cast-iron grill pan with remaining 1 tablespoon oil, and heat over medium-high heat. Add peppers and onion; cook, turning occasionally, until softened and grill marks form, about 5 minutes.

Remove from pan, and place on a cutting board. Let cool slightly; coarsely chop. Transfer to a small bowl, and stir in cilantro and all remaining ingredients. Serve immediately, or cover and refrigerate for up to 1 day.

FRIED COCONUT CATFISH NUGGETS

*We love the sweet crunch that coconut gives
these bite-sized pieces of fried catfish.*

MAKES 4 TO 6 SERVINGS

3 large eggs, lightly beaten
1½ cups all-purpose flour
1½ cups sweetened flaked coconut
1½ cups panko (Japanese bread crumbs)
1½ teaspoons plus ⅛ teaspoon kosher salt, divided
¼ teaspoon ground black pepper
1½ pounds catfish fillets, cut into 1-inch pieces
Vegetable oil, for frying
⅔ cup orange marmalade
2 tablespoons water
1 tablespoon chopped green onion
1 tablespoon fresh ground chili paste*
1 teaspoon soy sauce

*We used Sambal Oelek

In a shallow dish, place eggs. In another shallow dish, stir together flour, coconut, bread crumbs, 1½ teaspoons salt, and pepper. Working in batches, dip fish in eggs, letting excess drip off. Dredge in flour mixture, shaking off excess.

In a large cast-iron skillet, pour oil to a depth of 2 inches, and heat over medium heat until a deep-fry thermometer registers 350°. Fry fish in batches, turning occasionally, until golden brown, about 2 minutes. Remove fish using a slotted spoon, and let drain on paper towels.

In a medium bowl, whisk together marmalade, 2 tablespoons water, green onion, chili paste, soy sauce, and remaining ⅛ teaspoon salt. Serve with catfish.

CATFISH-CORNBREAD CAKES

These cakes will make the perfect appetizer at your next party.

MAKES 4 SERVINGS

2½   cups crumbled cornbread
¼   cup chopped green onion
¼   cup finely chopped celery
1   teaspoon hot sauce
¼   teaspoon kosher salt
¼   teaspoon ground black
     pepper
1½   cups cooked coarsely
     flaked catfish fillets
6   tablespoons mayonnaise,
     divided
1   large egg
¼   cup vegetable oil
Black-Eyed Pea Relish
     (recipe follows)

BLACK-EYED PEA RELISH
1   (15-ounce) can black-eyed
     peas, rinsed and drained
1   (4-ounce) jar diced
     pimientos, drained
⅓   cup chopped green onion
2   tablespoons distilled white
     vinegar
1   tablespoon vegetable oil
¼   teaspoon kosher salt
¼   teaspoon ground black
     pepper

Line a baking sheet with parchment paper.

In a medium bowl, stir together cornbread, green onion, celery, hot sauce, salt, and pepper. Add fish, tossing gently to combine.

In a small bowl, whisk together 5 tablespoons mayonnaise and egg. Add to fish mixture, stirring gently to combine. Add remaining 1 tablespoon mayonnaise, if needed. Shape mixture into 12 (2-inch) patties. Place on prepared pan; cover and refrigerate for 30 minutes.

In a medium cast-iron skillet, heat oil over medium-high heat.

Reduce heat to medium. Add half of cakes, and cook until golden brown, about 2 minutes per side. Repeat procedure with remaining cakes. Serve with Black-Eyed Pea Relish.

FOR BLACK-EYED PEA RELISH In a medium bowl, stir together all ingredients. Serve immediately, or cover and refrigerate for up to 1 day.

5

BLACKENED CATFISH PO'BOYS

Eating these po' boys is like taking a trip to New Orleans.

— MAKES 4 —

1   tablespoon garlic powder
2   teaspoons kosher salt
2   teaspoons paprika
½   teaspoon ground red pepper
½   teaspoon dried thyme
4   (6-ounce) catfish fillets
4   tablespoons vegetable oil,
      divided
Spicy-Sweet Tartar Sauce
      (recipe follows)
4   (6-inch) slices French bread,
      split lengthwise
Lettuce, tomato, and potato
      chips, to serve

SPICY-SWEET TARTAR SAUCE
¾   cup mayonnaise
½   cup chopped spicy sweet
      pickles
¼   cup sour cream
1   tablespoon chopped
      fresh dill
½   teaspoon lemon zest
1   teaspoon fresh lemon juice
⅛   teaspoon kosher salt
⅛   teaspoon ground black
      pepper

In a small bowl, stir together garlic powder, salt, paprika, red pepper, and thyme. Lightly brush fish with 2 tablespoons oil. Sprinkle both sides of fish with garlic powder mixture.

In a large cast-iron skillet, heat remaining 2 tablespoons oil over medium-high heat. Add fish; cook until fish can be easily turned with a spatula, about 3 minutes. Turn fish; cook until fish is opaque and flakes easily with a fork, about 2 minutes more.

Spread Spicy-Sweet Tartar Sauce onto cut sides of bread. Top with fish, lettuce, and tomato. Serve with potato chips.

FOR SPICY-SWEET TARTAR SAUCE In a small bowl, whisk together all ingredients. Serve immediately, or cover and refrigerate for up to 3 days.

5 WAYS WITH
BANANA PUDDING

IN A REGION well known for its showpiece desserts, banana pudding stands out as a Southern favorite. This creamy, comfort-filled dish is an expectation at any Southern gathering where dessert is even a remote possibility.

Bananas first made their way to America from the Caribbean through the Southern port cities of New Orleans and Charleston. Exotic for the times, this ingredient excited the imaginations of many early 20th century home cooks. Variations found in newspaper recipe submissions and church cookbooks incorporated just about everything into banana puddings, from ladyfingers to sponge cake.

Mid-century versions opted for quick ingredient substitutions, a trend that convenience-food marketers jumped on. Jell-O Instant Pudding & Pie Filling replaced homemade custard, whipped toppings such as Cool Whip replaced the meringue or whipped cream, and Nabisco 'Nilla Wafers took over for their cakier counterparts.

But the beauty of banana pudding is that there's no such thing as bad banana pudding. Whether it's homemade from top to bottom or whipped up in twenty minutes with storebought staples, it's still perfectly delicious, spoonful after spoonful.

1

CLASSIC BANANA PUDDING

Layered with homemade custard and topped with
billowy meringue, this is banana pudding at its best.

MAKES 12 SERVINGS

2⅓ cups sugar, divided
½ cup all-purpose flour
¼ teaspoon kosher salt
3½ cups whole milk, divided
8 large eggs, separated
1 tablespoon unsalted
butter
1½ teaspoons vanilla extract
1 (11-ounce) box vanilla
wafers
6 medium bananas, sliced
1 teaspoon cream of
tartar
Garnish: vanilla wafers

Preheat oven to 350°.

In a medium bowl, whisk together 1 cup sugar, flour, and salt. Whisk in ½ cup milk and egg yolks. In a large saucepan, place remaining 3 cups milk. Bring to a simmer over medium heat, stirring frequently. Whisk 1 cup hot milk into egg mixture. Whisk egg mixture into remaining hot milk in saucepan. Bring to a boil over medium heat, stirring constantly. Cook, stirring constantly, until thickened, about 3 minutes more. Remove from heat. Add butter and vanilla, stirring until butter melts. Let cool slightly.

Arrange vanilla wafers in the bottom of a 13x9-inch baking dish; top with banana slices. Pour pudding over bananas.

In a large bowl, beat egg whites and cream of tartar with a mixer at high speed until soft peaks form. Gradually add remaining 1⅓ cups sugar, beating until stiff peaks form. Spoon over pudding, spreading to seal edges.

Bake until lightly browned, about 10 minutes. Garnish edges of pudding with vanilla wafers, if desired. Let cool for 10 minutes before serving.

BANANA PUDDING DIP

Quick and easy, this fun twist on banana pudding is the perfect sweet appetizer.

MAKES 6 SERVINGS

1   (3-ounce) box vanilla
    cook-and-serve
    pudding mix
2   cups whole milk
½   (8-ounce) package
    cream cheese, softened
½   cup frozen whipped
    topping, thawed
2   tablespoons
    confectioners' sugar
⅔   cup mashed banana

Garnish: whipped topping,
    banana slices, crushed
    vanilla wafers

Vanilla wafers and graham
    crackers, to serve

In a medium saucepan, bring pudding mix and milk to a boil over medium heat, stirring frequently. Reduce heat to low; add cream cheese, stirring until smooth. Pour into a medium bowl; cover and refrigerate until chilled.

Add whipped topping and confectioners' sugar, whisking until smooth. Stir in banana.

Garnish with whipped topping, banana slices, and crushed vanilla wafers, if desired. Serve with vanilla wafers and graham crackers.

BANANA PUDDING FILLED CUPCAKES

There's no better surprise than a cupcake filled with banana pudding.

MAKES 12

FILLING
- 3 tablespoons sugar
- 1½ tablespoons all-purpose flour
- ⅛ teaspoon kosher salt
- 1 cup whole milk, divided
- 2 large egg yolks
- 2 teaspoons unsalted butter
- ½ teaspoon vanilla extract

CUPCAKES
- ½ cup unsalted butter, softened
- 1 cup sugar
- 2 large eggs
- 2 cups all-purpose flour
- 2 teaspoons baking powder
- ¼ teaspoon kosher salt
- ⅔ cup whole buttermilk
- ½ cup mashed banana
- ½ teaspoon vanilla extract
- ¾ cup sweetened whipped cream
- 1 medium banana, sliced

Garnish: sweetened whipped cream, banana slices, crushed and whole vanilla wafers

FOR FILLING In a small bowl, whisk together sugar, flour, and salt. Whisk in ¼ cup milk and egg yolks. In a small saucepan, place remaining ¾ cup milk. Bring to a simmer over medium heat, stirring frequently. Whisk ¼ cup hot milk into egg mixture. Whisk egg mixture into remaining hot milk in saucepan. Bring to a boil over medium heat, whisking constantly. Cook, stirring constantly, until thickened, about 1 minute more.

Remove from heat. Add butter and vanilla, stirring until butter melts. Let pudding cool for 10 minutes. Cover with plastic wrap, and refrigerate until cold, about 1 hour or up to 2 days. Preheat oven to 350°. Line muffin cups with paper liners.

FOR CUPCAKES In a large bowl, beat butter and sugar with a mixer at medium speed until fluffy, stopping to scrape sides of bowl. Add eggs, one at a time, beating well after each addition. In a small bowl, whisk together flour, baking powder, and salt. Gradually add flour mixture to butter mixture alternately with buttermilk, beginning and ending with flour mixture. Stir in mashed banana and vanilla. Spoon batter into prepared muffin cups, filling about two-thirds full.

Bake until a wooden pick inserted in center comes out clean, about 20 minutes. Let cool completely in pan.

Remove cupcakes from pan. Using a serrated knife, slice tops from cupcakes. Remove a small amount of cake from center of each cupcake. Fill center with about 2 teaspoons filling and 2 teaspoons whipped cream. Top with 2 or 3 banana slices. Cover with cupcake tops. Garnish with whipped cream, banana slices, and vanilla wafers, if desired.

4

BANANA PUDDING BARS

These creamy bars are everything we love
about banana pudding in a grab-and-go form.

───────── MAKES ABOUT 18 ─────────

2   cups graham cracker
     crumbs
1½   cups gingersnap crumbs
½   cup unsalted butter,
     melted
3   cups whole milk, divided
1½   cups fresh banana purée
     (2 or 3 medium bananas)
1   cup granulated sugar,
     divided
2   teaspoons vanilla
     extract
3   teaspoons unflavored
     gelatin
8   large egg yolks
½   cup all-purpose flour
1½   cups heavy whipping
     cream
¼   cup confectioners' sugar
Garnish: mini vanilla wafers

Preheat oven to 350°. In a medium bowl, combine graham cracker crumbs, gingersnap crumbs, and melted butter. Press mixture into bottom of a 13x9-inch baking pan.

Bake until golden brown, about 10 minutes. Let cool completely on a wire rack.

In a medium saucepan, combine 2¾ cups milk, banana purée, ¾ cup granulated sugar, and vanilla. Cook over medium heat, whisking frequently, until mixture comes to a boil. Remove from heat.

In a small bowl, combine gelatin and remaining ¼ cup milk. Let stand for 5 minutes. In a medium bowl, whisk together egg yolks, flour, and remaining ¼ cup granulated sugar.

Add gelatin mixture to milk mixture, whisking to combine. Ladle about 1 cup hot milk mixture into yolk mixture, whisking constantly. Pour egg mixture into remaining milk mixture, whisking constantly. Cook over medium-high heat, stirring constantly, until mixture begins to thicken. Gently boil for 2 minutes. Remove from heat, and strain through a fine-mesh sieve. Spread onto prepared crust. Let cool to room temperature. Refrigerate for at least 6 hours.

In a medium bowl, beat cream and confectioners' sugar with a mixer at medium-high speed until medium peaks form. Spread onto cooled custard. Cut into bars. Garnish with a mini vanilla wafer, if desired. Cover and refrigerate for up to 5 days.

BANANA PUDDING POKE CAKE

Cake drenched in banana pudding? Plan on having seconds.

— MAKES 10 TO 12 SERVINGS —

CAKE

- ¾ cup unsalted butter, softened
- 1½ cups sugar
- 3 large eggs
- 2⅔ cups all-purpose flour
- 2½ teaspoons baking powder
- ¼ teaspoon baking soda
- ¼ teaspoon kosher salt
- 1 cup whole buttermilk
- ½ cup mashed banana
- ½ teaspoon vanilla extract

PUDDING

- 1 cup sugar
- ½ cup all-purpose flour
- ¼ teaspoon kosher salt
- 3½ cups whole milk, divided
- 8 large egg yolks
- 1 tablespoon unsalted butter
- 1½ teaspoons vanilla extract
- 3 medium bananas, sliced
- 4 cups frozen whipped topping, thawed
- ½ cup crushed vanilla wafers

Garnish: whole vanilla wafers

Preheat oven to 350°. Spray a 13x9-inch baking dish with baking spray with flour.

FOR CAKE In a large bowl, beat butter and sugar with a mixer at medium speed until fluffy, 3 to 4 minutes, stopping to scrape sides of bowl. Add eggs, one at a time, beating well after each addition.

In a medium bowl, whisk together flour, baking powder, baking soda, and salt. Gradually add flour mixture to butter mixture alternately with buttermilk, beginning and ending with flour mixture, beating just until combined after each addition. Add mashed banana and vanilla, beating just until combined. Spread into prepared pan.

Bake until a wooden pick inserted in center comes out clean, about 28 minutes. Let cool for 5 minutes. Using the handle of a wooden spoon, poke holes in warm cake.

FOR PUDDING In a medium bowl, whisk together sugar, flour, and salt. Whisk in ½ cup milk and egg yolks. In a large saucepan, place remaining 3 cups milk. Bring to a simmer over medium heat, stirring frequently. Whisk 1 cup hot milk into egg mixture. Whisk egg mixture into remaining hot milk in saucepan. Bring to a boil over medium heat, stirring constantly. Cook, stirring constantly, until thickened, about 3 minutes. Remove from heat. Add butter and vanilla, stirring until butter is melted. Let cool for 10 minutes, stirring occasionally. Pour over cake. Cover and refrigerate until chilled, about 4 hours.

Uncover; top with sliced bananas, and spread with whipped topping. Sprinkle with crushed vanilla wafers. Garnish with whole vanilla wafers around edges of dish, if desired.

5 WAYS WITH

PEAS & BEANS

THEY SAY YOU CAN TELL where a Southerner hails from by his or her preference in field peas and beans, the humble legumes that have fed the region in good times and bad. In the Lowcountry, folks make their New Year's Day Hoppin' John with Sea Island red peas. In the hills of Kentucky, the locals crumble cornbread into soup beans (pinto beans cooked in a soupy broth) to soak up the potlikker. To the west in Emerson, Arkansas, purple hull peas are celebrated at their own festival each June. When it comes to peas and beans, we love them all.

One of the earliest chores for many a Southern child was shelling peas. Sitting on a back porch, balancing a colander on your knees as you listened to your grandparents' wisdom was a right of passage.

Today is the best of times to be a lover of field peas and beans in the South. With the resurgence of farmers' markets, many fresh varieties are available throughout the summer. Bold pink-eye peas, pale zipper peas, delicate lady peas, and colorful cranberry beans appear regularly at local markets. And the one objection to field peas and beans has been removed. Today they come shelled. But if you get the chance to shell your own, take it. Sometimes it's nice to sit for a spell, and just shell.

1

CLASSIC BUTTERBEANS

*Many a Southern child learned about life sitting on the
back porch shelling butterbeans with their grandmother.*

— MAKES ABOUT 6 SERVINGS —

1½ **pounds shelled fresh
    butterbeans**
4   **cups low-sodium
    chicken broth**
1   **ham hock**
1   **Vidalia onion, peeled
    and quartered**
4   **cloves garlic, peeled**
3   **bay leaves**
3   **dried chile peppers**
Ground black pepper

In a large saucepan, place butterbeans. Add broth to cover.
Add ham hock, onion, garlic, bay leaves, and chile peppers.
Add water, if necessary, to cover beans.

Cook over high heat until mixture comes to a boil.
Reduce heat, and simmer, stirring occasionally, until
tender, 45 minutes to 1 hour. Season to taste with pepper.

BUTTERBEAN *AND* CORN SALAD

A light and fresh dressing transforms crisp, blanched butterbeans and sweet corn into the ultimate summer salad.

——— MAKES ABOUT 6 SERVINGS ———

1 **pound shelled fresh butterbeans**

2½ **cups fresh corn kernels (from about 5 large ears corn)**

⅓ **cup chopped red onion**

2 **tablespoons chopped fresh thyme**

1 **(4-ounce) jar diced pimientos, drained**

¼ **cup fresh lemon juice**

3 **tablespoons canola oil**

¾ **teaspoon kosher salt**

¼ **teaspoon ground black pepper**

Garnish: cooked bacon slices, fresh thyme

Fill a large saucepan halfway full with water, and bring to a boil over medium-high heat. Add butterbeans; cook for 1 minute. Place in a colander. Rinse under cold running water; drain well.

In a medium bowl, combine butterbeans, corn, onion, thyme, and pimientos. In a small bowl, whisk together lemon juice, oil, salt, and pepper. Pour over corn mixture, stirring to combine. Let stand for at least 10 minutes, or cover and refrigerate for up to 2 days. Garnish with bacon and thyme, if desired.

3

A MESS OF FIELD PEAS
WITH HAM HOCKS

How many peas does it take to make a mess of peas?
Whatever it takes to feed your family.

MAKES 6 TO 8 SERVINGS

4   cups shelled fresh pink-eyed peas or other field peas
1   cup water
1   cup chicken broth
6   ounces smoked ham hocks, cut into ¼-inch slices
4   sprigs fresh thyme, leaves stripped and reserved
½   teaspoon kosher salt
⅛   teaspoon ground red pepper
Garnish: fresh thyme sprigs

In a large saucepan, combine peas, 1 cup water, and broth. Add ham hocks, thyme leaves, salt, and red pepper. Bring to a boil over medium-high heat.

Cover and reduce heat to a simmer. Cook until peas are very tender, 20 to 25 minutes. Garnish with thyme, if desired.

ROASTED FIELD PEA SALAD

Ever tried roasted peas? They're a delightful combination of crispy and tender—like miniature baked potatoes.

─── MAKES 6 SERVINGS ───

4   cups fresh crowder peas
2   tablespoons olive oil
1   teaspoon garlic powder
½   teaspoon kosher salt
¼   teaspoon ground black pepper
1   head green leaf lettuce, chopped
1   (4-ounce) bag fresh arugula
2   cups diced ham
2   cups halved grape tomatoes
Cheddar-Pecan Cornbread Croutons
     (recipe follows)
Herbed Buttermilk Dressing (recipe follows)

CHEDDAR-PECAN CORNBREAD CROUTONS
¼   cup unsalted butter, softened
2   cups self-rising cornmeal mix
1½   cups whole milk
¼   cup melted unsalted butter
1   large egg, lightly beaten
1   teaspoon garlic powder
1½   cups shredded sharp Cheddar cheese
1   cup finely chopped pecans

HERBED BUTTERMILK DRESSING
1   cup whole buttermilk
1   cup mayonnaise
1   cup sour cream
2   tablespoons white wine vinegar
2   tablespoons chopped fresh dill
2   tablespoons chopped fresh chives
2   tablespoons chopped fresh parsley
1   teaspoon garlic powder
1   teaspoon onion powder
¾   teaspoon kosher salt
½   teaspoon ground black pepper

Preheat oven to 400°. Line a rimmed baking sheet with foil. In a medium bowl, combine peas, oil, garlic powder, salt, and pepper, tossing to coat. Transfer mixture to prepared pan. Bake until crispy, 20 to 25 minutes.

Divide lettuce, arugula, ham, and tomatoes among 6 salad plates. Top with roasted peas and Cheddar-Pecan Cornbread Croutons. Serve with Herbed Buttermilk Dressing.

FOR CHEDDAR-PECAN CORNBREAD CROUTONS
Preheat oven to 450°. Place softened butter in a 13x9-inch baking pan. Place pan in oven for 2 to 3 minutes until butter is melted and pan is hot.

In a large bowl, whisk together cornmeal mix, milk, melted butter, egg, and garlic powder. Stir in cheese and pecans. Spoon batter into hot pan.

Bake until golden brown, about 20 minutes. Let cool completely on a wire rack. Cut cornbread into 1-inch cubes. Spray a large rimmed baking sheet with cooking spray. Place cornbread in a single layer on baking sheet. Bake until lightly browned, about 10 minutes.

FOR HERBED BUTTERMILK DRESSING In a medium bowl, whisk together buttermilk, mayonnaise, sour cream, and vinegar. Add dill, chives, parsley, garlic powder, onion powder, salt, and pepper, stirring to combine. Cover and refrigerate for up to 1 week.

5

FRESH FIELD PEA SALSA

Infused with fresh Latin flavors,
this Southern-style salsa is a hit at potlucks.

MAKES ABOUT 12 CUPS

2   cups fresh baby lima beans,
    blanched (see note)
2   cups fresh lady peas, blanched
2   cups fresh pink-eyed peas,
    blanched
3   large ripe tomatoes, seeded
    and chopped
1   large yellow bell pepper,
    seeded and chopped
1   poblano pepper, seeded
    and chopped
1   jalapeño pepper, seeded
    and minced
1   cup finely chopped red onion
¼   cup chopped fresh cilantro
¼   cup olive oil
¼   cup fresh lime juice
2   tablespoons white wine vinegar
2   teaspoons garlic powder
½   teaspoon salt
¼   teaspoon ground black pepper
Tortilla chips

In a large bowl, combine lima beans, peas, tomatoes, peppers, onion, cilantro, oil, lime juice, vinegar, garlic powder, salt, and black pepper.

Cover and refrigerate for at least 1 hour. Serve with tortilla chips.

NOTE: *To blanch peas and beans, cook in boiling salted water for 2 to 3 minutes. Drain.*

5 WAYS WITH

CORNBREAD

CHANCES ARE, there's one special way you like your cornbread, which is, of course, the best way to eat it. It's probably the way your mother or grandmother ate it before you.

Perhaps you prefer a mix of yellow and white cornmeal, or you wouldn't dream of making it without buttermilk. Maybe your cornbread is best for sopping up potlikker. But no matter how you like to eat cornbread, the very first step in making it is greasing a cast-iron skillet. Be it lard or bacon grease, shortening or vegetable oil, the fat goes in until it sizzles on the hot iron. And it's in that sizzle, that initial moment of contact, when a crisp and crunchy crust is born.

That buttery crust, coupled with a fluffy interior, makes this unassuming quick bread so beloved. We'll eat it speckled with green onion, corn, and bacon, fried as hush puppies, or saved for dessert and swimming in syrup or honey.

But ultimately, we love cornbread because it speaks of home. It speaks of that place that we create and re-create around kitchen stoves and kitchen tables. Cornbread is community food. It's prepared from your grandmother's recipe, passed down with her hearth-blackened cast-iron skillet. Or made from your next-door neighbor's recipe, taped to a Tupperware dish of chili. Cornbread is comfort—a gift of food that is best when shared.

1

CLASSIC SOUTHERN CORNBREAD

Whatever your skillet size, we've got the perfect recipe for you.

─────── MAKES 1 SKILLET ───────

FOR AN 8-INCH SKILLET

1	tablespoon canola oil
1	cup plain white or yellow cornmeal
½	cup all-purpose flour
1½	teaspoons baking powder
¾	teaspoon kosher salt
1¼	cups whole buttermilk
3	tablespoons unsalted butter, melted
1	large egg

FOR A 10-INCH SKILLET

2	tablespoons canola oil
2	cups plain white or yellow cornmeal
1	cup all-purpose flour
1	tablespoon baking powder
1½	teaspoons kosher salt
2½	cups whole buttermilk
6	tablespoons unsalted butter, melted
2	large eggs

FOR A 12-INCH SKILLET

3	tablespoons canola oil
4	cups plain white or yellow cornmeal
2	cups all-purpose flour
2	tablespoons baking powder
1	tablespoon kosher salt
5	cups whole buttermilk
¾	cup unsalted butter, melted
4	large eggs

FOR AN 8-INCH SKILLET Preheat oven to 425°. Pour oil into a deep 8-inch cast-iron skillet. Place pan in oven until oil is very hot, about 8 minutes.

In a large bowl, whisk together cornmeal, flour, baking powder, and salt. In a medium bowl, whisk together buttermilk, melted butter, and egg. Make a well in center of dry ingredients. Add buttermilk mixture; stir until combined. Carefully pour batter into hot oil.

Bake until golden brown and a wooden pick inserted in center comes out clean, about 25 minutes.

FOR A 10-INCH SKILLET Follow directions above using a 10-inch skillet; bake until golden brown and a wooden pick inserted in center comes out clean, about 27 minutes.

FOR A 12-INCH SKILLET Follow directions above using a 12-inch skillet; bake until golden brown and a wooden pick inserted in center comes out clean, about 35 minutes.

BACON-CHEDDAR CORNBREAD

The crispy edges and bacon-Cheddar flavor make this cornbread hard to beat.

MAKES 1 (10-INCH) SKILLET

6   slices thick-cut bacon,
      cut into ½-inch pieces
1   cup chopped yellow
      onion
½   cup fresh or frozen corn
      kernels
2   cups plain yellow
      cornmeal
1   cup all-purpose flour
1   tablespoon sugar
1   tablespoon baking
      powder
1½   teaspoons kosher salt,
      divided
1¼   cups shredded sharp
      yellow Cheddar cheese,
      divided
2   cups whole buttermilk
2   large eggs
Garnish: cooked and
      crumbled bacon
Butter, to serve

Preheat oven to 400°. In a deep 10-inch cast-iron skillet, cook bacon over medium heat until crisp, about 10 minutes. Remove bacon using a slotted spoon, and let drain on paper towels. Remove all but 2 tablespoons bacon drippings from skillet; reserve remaining drippings.

Add onion and corn to skillet. Cook, stirring frequently, until tender, about 3 minutes. Remove onion mixture from skillet. Add 2 tablespoons reserved drippings to skillet; reduce heat to medium-low.

In a large bowl, whisk together cornmeal, flour, sugar, baking powder, and 1 teaspoon salt. Stir in 1 cup cheese.

In a medium bowl, whisk together buttermilk, eggs, and remaining reserved drippings. Make a well in center of dry ingredients. Add buttermilk mixture; stir until just combined. Stir in bacon and onion mixture. Sprinkle remaining ½ teaspoon salt in skillet. Carefully pour batter into hot drippings. Top with remaining ¼ cup cheese.

Bake until golden brown and a wooden pick inserted in center comes out clean, about 30 minutes. Garnish with bacon, if desired. Serve with butter.

3

BARBECUE-STUFFED CORN MUFFINS

Cornbread and barbecue are a natural combination.
Aren't you glad we thought of putting them together?

— MAKES 12 —

1 **cup stone-ground white or yellow cornmeal**
1 **cup all-purpose flour**
2 **teaspoons baking powder**
1 **teaspoon kosher salt**
½ **teaspoon baking soda**
1 **cup canned cream-style corn**
¾ **cup whole buttermilk**
¼ **cup unsalted butter, melted**
1 **large egg**
1 **cup prepared pulled pork**
¼ **cup barbecue sauce, plus more to serve**

Preheat oven to 425°. Place a 12-cup muffin pan in oven to preheat.

In a large bowl, whisk together cornmeal, flour, baking powder, salt, and baking soda.

In a medium bowl, stir together corn, buttermilk, melted butter, and egg. Make a well in center of dry ingredients. Add corn mixture, stirring just until combined.

In a small bowl, stir together pulled pork and barbecue sauce until combined.

Carefully remove hot pan from oven. Spray with cooking spray. Spoon 1 tablespoon batter in each muffin cup. (Batter should sizzle in hot pan.) Place 1 tablespoon pork mixture in center of each batter-filled cup. Top each with another 1 tablespoon batter.

Bake until golden brown, about 18 minutes. Quickly and carefully remove muffins from pan. Place on a wire rack, and let cool slightly. Serve warm with barbecue sauce, if desired.

JALAPEÑO GOAT CHEESE CORNBREAD

This showstopping cornbread gets a rich flavor boost from tangy goat cheese.

———————— MAKES 1 (12-INCH) SKILLET ————————

5	fresh jalapeño peppers, halved
3	tablespoons canola oil
4	cups plain white or yellow cornmeal
2	cups all-purpose flour
½	cup chopped fresh jalapeño pepper
2	tablespoons baking powder
1	tablespoon kosher salt
5	cups whole buttermilk
¾	cup unsalted butter, melted
4	large eggs
2	(4-ounce) packages goat cheese, crumbled
⅓	cup shredded mild Cheddar cheese

Preheat oven to 425°. Heat a 12-inch cast-iron skillet over medium-high heat. Add halved jalapeños to skillet. Cook until lightly charred on each side, about 2 minutes per side. Remove from skillet.

Pour oil into skillet. Place skillet in oven until oil is very hot, about 8 minutes.

In a large bowl, whisk together cornmeal, flour, chopped jalapeño, baking powder, and salt.

In a medium bowl, whisk together buttermilk, melted butter, and eggs. Make a well in center of dry ingredients; add buttermilk mixture, stirring until combined. Stir in goat cheese. Carefully pour batter into hot oil in skillet. Sprinkle with Cheddar. Top with charred jalapeño, cut side up.

Bake until golden brown and a wooden pick inserted in center comes out clean, about 35 minutes.

BROWNED BUTTER CORNBREAD *with* THYME

Humble cornbread gets an elegant upgrade with fresh herbs and golden honey.

———— MAKES 1 (12-INCH) SKILLET ————

¾   cup unsalted butter
10 sprigs fresh thyme
3   tablespoons canola oil
4   cups plain white or yellow
    cornmeal
2   cups all-purpose flour
¼   cup fresh thyme leaves
2   tablespoons baking powder
1   tablespoon kosher salt
1   tablespoon ground black
    pepper
4   cups whole buttermilk
4   large eggs
⅔   cup honey
Honey and butter, to serve

Preheat oven to 400°. In a 12-inch cast-iron skillet, melt butter over medium heat. Add thyme sprigs; cook until butter starts to brown, 3 to 4 minutes. Pour butter into a medium bowl; discard thyme. Wipe skillet clean.

Add oil to skillet. Place skillet in oven until oil is very hot, about 8 minutes.

In a large bowl, whisk together cornmeal, flour, thyme leaves, baking powder, salt, and pepper. Add buttermilk, eggs, and honey to melted butter; whisk until combined. Make a well in center of dry ingredients; add buttermilk mixture, stirring until combined. Carefully pour batter into hot oil in skillet.

Bake until golden brown and a wooden pick inserted in center comes out clean, 35 to 40 minutes. Serve with honey and butter, if desired.

5 WAYS WITH
COLLARD GREENS

SIMMERING ALL DAY on the back of the stove in the largest pot in the house, collard greens are the backbone of Southern nutrition—and darn if they aren't delicious. Whether eaten with black-eyed peas for New Year's Day or as a side at a family potluck, collard greens anchor tables around the South.

Flavor them as you please, with fatback or a ham hock, onions or garlic, vinegar or pepper sauce. It's hard to find a wrong way to eat greens.

The practice of cooking them low and slow was a traditional African method that continued in the kitchens of slave quarters on plantations. The nourishing liquid from the boiled greens, or "potlikker," provided vital nutrition. As with many native foods and cooking practices, this method of preparing collard greens made its way into the kitchens of the plantation houses themselves.

Collard greens are such a large part of Southern cuisine, in fact, that South Carolina made them their official state vegetable, and festivals are held in cities like Atlanta and Savannah to celebrate the leafy greens. Once you've had them, you understand why: Nothing beats a mess o' greens swimming in potlikker—except maybe a wedge of cornbread to sop up all the goodness.

CLASSIC COLLARD GREENS

Bourbon adds a rich sweetness to this classic Southern side.
Substitute two tablespoons brown sugar, if you prefer.

——————— MAKES 8 TO 10 SERVINGS ———————

1   **tablespoon vegetable oil**
1   **large yellow onion, chopped**
3   **cloves garlic, smashed**
1   **smoked ham hock**
¾   **cup bourbon**
½   **cup apple cider vinegar**
8   **cups low-sodium chicken broth**
1   **tablespoon seasoned salt**
1   **teaspoon ground black pepper**
½   **teaspoon crushed red pepper**
2   **pounds fresh collard greens, roughly chopped**

In a large Dutch oven, heat oil over medium-high heat. Add onion; cook, stirring occasionally, until translucent, about 5 minutes. Add garlic; cook until fragrant, about 1 minute. Add ham hock; cook, turning occasionally, to sear all sides.

Stir in bourbon and vinegar, and cook for 1 minute, scraping browned bits from bottom of pan with a wooden spoon. Add broth, salt, black pepper, and red pepper; bring to a boil. Reduce heat to medium. Add greens in batches, stirring to combine. Cover and cook until tender, about 1 hour.

2

COLLARD GREEN PIES

If you don't have the small skillets to make these single-serving pies, a 10-inch skillet will do.

──────── MAKES 6 (6-INCH) SKILLETS ────────

1	tablespoon vegetable oil
1	cup chopped green onion
1	clove garlic, minced
10	cups cooked collard greens, drained and finely chopped
3	large eggs, lightly beaten
1½	cups feta cheese, crumbled
1	cup cottage cheese
½	cup chopped fresh dill
½	cup chopped fresh parsley
2	teaspoons apple cider vinegar
1	teaspoon kosher salt
½	teaspoon crushed red pepper
¼	teaspoon ground black pepper
2	(14.1-ounce) packages refrigerated piecrusts, at room temperature
½	cup grated Parmesan cheese

Garnish: ground black pepper

Preheat oven to 375°. Spray 6 (6-inch) cast-iron skillets with cooking spray.

In a large skillet, heat oil over medium-high heat. Add green onion and garlic; cook until onion is tender, about 2 minutes.

In a large bowl, stir together onion mixture, collard greens, eggs, feta, cottage cheese, dill, parsley, vinegar, salt, red pepper, and black pepper.

On a lightly floured surface, unroll 1 piecrust. Lightly brush with water, and place another piecrust on top. Roll ⅛-inch thick. Cut 3 (5-inch) rounds, reserving scraps. Repeat process with remaining piecrusts. Roll each round into a 7-inch circle. Transfer rounds to prepared skillets, pressing into bottom and up sides. Fill each with 1 cup filling. Cut scraps into 4- to 6-inch strips, rerolling scraps as necessary. Arrange 6 to 8 dough strips of various widths on top of each skillet in a lattice pattern. Gently press to seal and trim sides. Sprinkle each with about 1½ tablespoons Parmesan.

Bake on bottom third of oven until golden brown, about 30 minutes. Let cool for 5 minutes before serving. Garnish with pepper, if desired.

COLLARD SALAD *with* WARM BACON VINAIGRETTE

This smoky dressing transforms greens into a standout salad.

—————— MAKES 4 SERVINGS ——————

½ cup apple cider vinegar

1 tablespoon sugar

2½ teaspoons kosher salt, divided

1 large red onion, thinly sliced

1 tablespoon extra-virgin olive oil

3 slices thick-cut bacon, cut into ¼-inch pieces

2½ tablespoons sherry vinegar

1 tablespoon whole-grain mustard

1 teaspoon chopped fresh thyme

5 cups chopped fresh collard greens

1 Fuji apple, cored and thinly sliced

½ cup chopped pecans

½ teaspoon ground black pepper

In a small saucepan, bring apple cider vinegar, sugar, and 1½ teaspoons salt to a boil over medium-high heat. Remove from heat; add onion, stirring well. Let stand at room temperature for 1 hour. Cover and refrigerate for up to 2 weeks.

In a medium skillet, heat oil over medium-high heat. Add bacon; cook until crispy, about 5 minutes. Remove from heat, and stir in sherry vinegar, mustard, and thyme until combined.

In a large bowl, toss together collard greens, apple, pecans, pepper, ¾ cup pickled red onions, warm vinaigrette, and remaining 1 teaspoon salt. Serve immediately. Reserve remaining onion for another use.

COLLARD GREENS *AND* SMOKED SAUSAGE STEW

*Packed with greens and smoked sausage,
this hearty soup will warm you down to your toes.*

———————————— MAKES 6 TO 8 SERVINGS ————————————

1   **(1-pound) package smoked
    sausage, thinly sliced***
2   **cups chopped yellow onion**
1   **cup chopped green bell pepper**
1   **tablespoon minced
    fresh garlic**
4   **cups chopped fresh collard
    greens, stems removed**
1   **(28-ounce) can plum tomatoes,
    drained and crushed**
6   **cups low-sodium chicken broth**
2½ **teaspoons kosher salt**
2   **teaspoons sugar**
¼   **teaspoon ground black pepper**
2   **teaspoons apple cider vinegar**
1   **teaspoon hot sauce**

**We used Conecuh brand hickory-smoked
sausage.*

Heat a large nonstick skillet over medium-high heat. Add sausage, onion, pepper, and garlic to skillet. Cook, stirring frequently, until sausage is browned and vegetables are tender, about 6 minutes.

Transfer sausage mixture to a 6-quart slow cooker. Add collards, tomatoes, broth, salt, sugar, and pepper.

Cover and cook on low for 6 hours, or on high for 4 hours. Stir in vinegar and hot sauce just before serving.

QUICK SKILLET COLLARDS

*This easy side dish comes together in less than
20 minutes, making it perfect for weeknight suppers.*

MAKES 4 TO 6 SERVINGS

1	tablespoon vegetable oil
2	shallots, quartered
1	cup diced country ham
1	clove garlic, minced
1	pound fresh collard greens, trimmed and thinly sliced
2	tablespoons cane syrup
½	teaspoon ground black pepper

In a 10-inch cast-iron skillet, heat oil over medium-high heat. Add shallots; cook, stirring frequently, until lightly browned, about 8 minutes.

Add ham; cook until crisp, about 3 minutes. Add garlic; cook for 1 minute. Add collards, cane syrup, and pepper; cook until crisp-tender, about 5 minutes.

5 WAYS WITH

SQUASH

THE EPITOME OF ABUNDANCE, squash overflows from Southern gardens every summer. Even those with the brownest of green thumbs find themselves with an almost limitless supply, sneaking the prolific vegetable into everything they can think of, from macaroni and cheese to pound cake. And those are just the ones they tell you about.

Along with its green cousin, zucchini, gold ol' yellow crookneck squash are delightful in all manner of recipes. Thanks to their thin skins, there's no peeling required, making these vegetables the friends of busy Southern cooks. Whether they're sliced into coins, boiled tender, and layered with cheese and crackers to create the quintessential casserole, quickly sautéed with fresh herbs for a light side dish, or charred in your favorite cast-iron skillet, the ways to enjoy squash are as endless as your harvest.

So before you sneak off to your neighbors' house under the cover of darkness to secretly drop a basket of squash on their doorstep, peruse these recipes and put your bounty of squash to a tasty good use.

CLASSIC SQUASH CASSEROLE

*Layered with tender squash, Cheddar, and buttery crackers,
this is comfort food at its finest.*

SERVES ABOUT 10

10 cups sliced yellow squash
(about 3 pounds)
1½ cups chopped yellow onion
3 cups water
3 cups chicken broth
1 cup shredded Cheddar
cheese, divided
½ cup sour cream
½ cup mayonnaise
2 tablespoons unsalted
butter, melted, divided
1 teaspoon kosher salt
½ teaspoon ground black
pepper
¼ teaspoon garlic powder
1 large egg, lightly beaten
1½ cups crushed buttery
round crackers, divided

Preheat oven to 350°. Spray a 2- to 2½-quart baking dish with cooking spray.

In a large Dutch oven, bring squash, onion, 3 cups water, and broth to a boil. Reduce heat to medium-low; simmer until squash is crisp-tender, about 7 minutes. Drain well.

In a large bowl, gently stir together squash mixture, ½ cup cheese, sour cream, mayonnaise, 1 tablespoon melted butter, salt, pepper, garlic powder, and egg. Spoon half of squash mixture into prepared dish, spreading evenly. Sprinkle with ¾ cup crushed crackers. Top with remaining squash mixture, remaining ¾ cup crushed crackers, and remaining ½ cup cheese. Drizzle with remaining 1 tablespoon melted butter.

Bake until cheese melts, about 25 minutes.

SKILLET ROASTED SQUASH

*This combination of simple and seasonal ingredients
brings out the fresh flavor of summer squash.*

2 tablespoons vegetable oil, divided

2 pounds medium yellow squash, halved lengthwise and cut crosswise

1 large Fresno chile pepper, sliced

½ teaspoon kosher salt

¼ teaspoon ground black pepper

¼ cup crumbled goat cheese

2 tablespoons torn fresh mint

1½ tablespoons panko (Japanese bread crumbs), toasted

Preheat oven to 425°. In a 12-inch cast-iron skillet, pour 1 tablespoon oil. Place skillet in oven until very hot, about 8 minutes.

In a large bowl, toss together squash, chile pepper, salt, pepper, and remaining 1 tablespoon oil. Carefully place squash in hot skillet, cut side down.

Bake until browned, about 8 minutes. Turn squash; bake until tender, about 6 minutes more. Remove from oven; sprinkle with goat cheese, mint, and bread crumbs.

3

ZUCCHINI BREAD *with* BUTTERMILK-LEMON GLAZE

*The bountiful blessing of Southern gardens, zucchini sneaks
its way into many an old Southern recipe, because we just can't bring
ourselves to waste it. This bread is a great way to use up your bumper crop.*

--- MAKES 1 (8X5-INCH) LOAF ---

2 cups all-purpose flour
¾ cup granulated sugar
½ cup toasted pecans, chopped
2 teaspoons baking powder
½ teaspoon baking soda
½ teaspoon ground nutmeg
½ teaspoon kosher salt
1 cup shredded zucchini
 (about 1 medium zucchini)
⅔ cup whole milk
⅓ cup unsalted butter, melted
2 teaspoons lemon zest
1 large egg
⅓ cup confectioners' sugar,
 sifted
2 teaspoons whole buttermilk
1 teaspoon fresh lemon juice

Preheat oven to 350°. Spray an 8x5-inch loaf pan with baking spray with flour.

In a large bowl, stir together flour, granulated sugar, pecans, baking powder, baking soda, nutmeg, and salt. Add zucchini, stirring to combine. In a small bowl, stir together milk, melted butter, zest, and egg. Pour over flour mixture, stirring just until moistened. Spoon batter into prepared pan.

Bake until a wooden pick inserted in center comes out clean, about 50 minutes. Let cool in pan for 10 minutes. Remove from pan, and let cool completely on a wire rack.

In a small bowl, stir together confectioners' sugar, buttermilk, and lemon juice until smooth. Drizzle over bread.

4

SQUASH SLAW

This tangy side dish is a great way to use up an abundance of squash.

MAKES 6 TO 8 SERVINGS

2 large yellow squash, grated and squeezed dry

2 large zucchini, grated and squeezed dry

2 carrots, grated

¼ cup finely chopped red bell pepper

2 green onions, finely chopped

½ cup distilled white vinegar

¼ cup sugar

½ teaspoon salt

½ teaspoon ground black pepper

¼ cup vegetable oil

In a medium bowl, combine squash, zucchini, carrots, bell pepper, and green onion. Set aside.

In a small bowl, combine vinegar, sugar, salt, and pepper. Whisk until sugar is dissolved. Gradually add oil, whisking until combined.

Add vinegar mixture to squash mixture, stirring to combine well. Cover and refrigerate for 1 hour.

SQUASH RIBBONS *WITH* TOMATO *AND* WHITE WINE BUTTER SAUCE

*Serve this elegant squash side dish
with your favorite grilled fish or chicken.*

— MAKES 6 SERVINGS —

2 medium yellow squash
3 medium zucchini
2 tablespoons extra-virgin
   olive oil
Tomato and White Wine Butter
   Sauce (recipe follows)
¼ cup toasted pine nuts
2 tablespoons drained capers

TOMATO AND WHITE WINE
   BUTTER SAUCE
1 cup dry white wine
1 shallot, finely chopped
1 teaspoon black peppercorns
8 tablespoons unsalted butter,
   cut into tablespoons
1 medium tomato, seeded and
   chopped

Using a vegetable peeler, peel squash and zucchini into ribbons, discarding seeds and core.

In a large nonstick skillet, heat oil over medium-high heat. Add squash and zucchini ribbons; cook, stirring frequently, until tender, 5 to 6 minutes.

Place ribbons in serving dish; spoon Tomato and White Wine Butter Sauce over ribbons. Top with pine nuts and capers. Serve immediately.

FOR TOMATO AND WHITE WINE BUTTER SAUCE In a medium saucepan, bring wine, shallot, and peppercorns to a simmer over medium-high heat. Cook until wine has reduced to about ¼ cup, 10 to 15 minutes.

Add butter, 1 tablespoon at a time, whisking until each addition is melted. Remove from heat; strain through a mesh sieve, discarding solids.

Return sauce to pan. Add tomato; cook, stirring frequently, over medium-low heat, until tomatoes are heated through, 3 to 4 minutes.

5 WAYS WITH
FRIED CHICKEN

HAVING FRIED CHICKEN for Sunday dinner used to be more of an occasion than it is today. Before the advent of take-out chicken, boneless fillets wedged between buns, and fast-food nuggets, really good fried chicken—delicately seasoned and pan-fried to a delicious crispiness—could only be experienced from the hands of a seasoned Southern cook, a master of the Gospel bird who had learned her way around a cast-iron skillet years before. When your mother or grandmother began heating up a big cast-iron skillet, you knew that magic was about to happen. Once the skillet was hot, she'd add a big dollop of Crisco shortening, waiting for it to melt. The chicken would be ready to go—a whole bird cut into eight pieces and then dredged in seasoned flour, dipped in buttermilk, and dredged in flour again. As she slid the pieces into the pan, you could hear the crackle and sizzle as the chicken hit the hot grease. There is no sound that is more Southern.

Fried chicken seemed to taste better in the old days—when it was served with rice and milk gravy made from the pan drippings. Not to mention the homemade biscuits. Treat yourself to one of these old-school recipes, and enjoy fried chicken like we used to in days gone by.

CLASSIC FRIED CHICKEN

*Crispy and tender, this is a recipe we
look forward to eating any day of the week.*

MAKES ABOUT 4 SERVINGS

Vegetable oil, for frying
3   cups all-purpose flour
1½ tablespoons kosher
    salt
1   tablespoon ground
    black pepper
2   teaspoons onion
    powder
2   cups whole buttermilk
1   (3-pound) whole
    chicken, cut into
    8 pieces

In a large Dutch oven, pour oil to halfway full, and heat over medium heat until a deep-fry thermometer registers 350°.

In a shallow dish, stir together flour, salt, pepper, and onion powder. In a medium bowl, place buttermilk. Working in batches, dredge chicken in flour mixture, shaking off excess. Dip in buttermilk, letting excess drip off; dredge in flour mixture again, pressing gently to adhere coating. Place chicken on a wire rack.

Fry chicken in batches, turning occasionally, until a meat thermometer inserted in thickest portion registers 165°, 6 to 12 minutes. Let drain on brown paper sackes or paper towels. Sprinkle with additional salt and pepper.

NASHVILLE-STYLE HOT CHICKEN WINGS

*Use more or less hot sauce to adjust the spiciness
of these picnic-perfect hot wings.*

─────── MAKES ABOUT 6 SERVINGS ───────

CHICKEN
Vegetable oil, for frying
3   cups all-purpose flour
1½ tablespoons kosher salt
1   tablespoon ground black
     pepper
2   teaspoons onion powder
2   cups whole buttermilk
3   pounds chicken wings,
     halved at the joint (tips
     left on)

SAUCE
**4 to 5 tablespoons hot pepper
     sauce**
2   tablespoons firmly
     packed light brown sugar
4   teaspoons distilled white
     vinegar
2   teaspoons smoked
     paprika
1   teaspoon kosher salt

FOR CHICKEN In a large Dutch oven, pour oil to halfway full, and heat over medium heat until a deep-fry thermometer registers 350°.

In a shallow dish, stir together flour, salt, pepper, and onion powder. In a medium bowl, place buttermilk. Working in batches, dredge chicken in flour mixture, shaking off excess. Dip in buttermilk, letting excess drip off; dredge in flour mixture again, pressing gently to adhere coating. Place chicken on a wire rack.

Fry chicken in batches, turning occasionally, until a meat thermometer inserted in thickest portion registers 165°, about 8 minutes. Let drain on paper towels. Place on a wire rack. Reserve ¾ cup cooking oil from pan for sauce.

FOR SAUCE In a medium bowl, whisk together reserved ¾ cup oil and all remaining ingredients. Brush over both sides of chicken. Serve remaining sauce with chicken.

3

PICKLE-BRINED CHICKEN TENDERS

Pickle juice adds a tangy flavor to this crispy fried chicken.

MAKES 8 SERVINGS

1 cup dill pickle juice
8 chicken tenderloins
Vegetable oil, for frying
1 cup all-purpose flour
1½ teaspoons kosher salt
1 teaspoon ground black pepper
¾ teaspoon onion powder
1 cup whole buttermilk
Dill pickle slices, buttermilk biscuits, honey mustard, to serve

In a resealable plastic bag, combine pickle juice and chicken. Seal bag; refrigerate for at least 6 hours or up to 8 hours.

In a small Dutch oven, pour oil to halfway full, and heat over medium heat until a deep-fry thermometer registers 350°.

In a shallow dish, stir together flour, salt, pepper, and onion powder. In a medium bowl, place buttermilk. Remove chicken from marinade; discard marinade. Working in batches, dredge chicken in flour mixture, shaking off excess. Dip in buttermilk, letting excess drip off; dredge in flour mixture again, pressing gently to adhere coating. Place chicken on a wire rack.

Fry chicken in batches, turning occasionally, until a meat thermometer inserted in thickest portion registers 165°, about 8 minutes. Let drain on paper towels. Sprinkle with additional salt and pepper. Serve with pickles, biscuits, and honey mustard, if desired.

4

SWEET TEA FRIED CHICKEN

Two Southern favorites come together to create one fantastic dish.

———— MAKES 4 TO 6 SERVINGS ————

½ **gallon plus 2 cups sweet tea, divided**

⅓ **cup plus 2 tablespoons kosher salt, divided**

1 **(3- to 4-pound) whole chicken, cut into pieces**

4 **cups all-purpose flour**

1 **teaspoon ground black pepper**

½ **teaspoon ground red pepper**

2 **cups whole buttermilk**

2 **tablespoons hot sauce**

5 **cups canola oil**

In a large glass or plastic bowl, stir together ½ gallon sweet tea and ⅓ cup salt until salt is dissolved. Add chicken pieces to sweet tea mixture. Cover and refrigerate for at least 8 hours or overnight.

Preheat oven to 350°. Spray the rack of a broiler pan with cooking spray; place rack in pan.

In a shallow dish, stir together flour, black pepper, red pepper, and remaining 2 tablespoons salt. In a medium bowl, combine buttermilk, hot sauce, and remaining 2 cups sweet tea. Remove chicken from sweet tea mixture. Dip chicken in buttermilk mixture, letting excess drip off; dredge in flour mixture, shaking off excess. Place chicken on a wire rack. Dredge chicken in flour mixture again, shaking off excess. Return to wire rack.

In a large cast-iron skillet, heat oil over medium-high heat until a deep-fry thermometer registers 350°. Working in batches, fry chicken, turning occasionally, until golden brown on all sides, 5 to 8 minutes. Place chicken on prepared pan.

Bake until a meat thermometer inserted in thickest portion registers 165°, 10 to 20 minutes.

RANCH-FRIED CHICKEN DRUMSTICKS

*These tasty drumsticks get a double hit of ranch flavor
from the breading and the tangy buttermilk dressing.*

MAKES 4 SERVINGS

1 **(1-ounce) packet ranch dressing mix**
3 **cups whole buttermilk, divided**
8 **small chicken drumsticks (about 2 pounds)**
Vegetable oil, for frying
3 **cups all-purpose flour**
1½ **tablespoons kosher salt**
1 **tablespoon ground black pepper**
2 **teaspoons onion powder**
1 **tablespoon chopped fresh chives**

In a large resealable plastic bag, combine dressing mix and 2 cups buttermilk. Seal bag, and shake until combined. Spoon ½ cup dressing into a small bowl. Cover and refrigerate. Add chicken to bag; seal and refrigerate for 8 hours. Drain chicken, discarding marinade. Lightly pat chicken with paper towels.

In a large Dutch oven, pour oil to halfway full, and heat over medium heat until a deep-fry thermometer registers 350°.

In a shallow dish, stir together flour, salt, pepper, and onion powder. In a medium bowl, place remaining 1 cup buttermilk. Working in batches, dredge chicken in flour mixture, shaking off excess. Dip in buttermilk, letting excess drip off; dredge in flour mixture again, pressing gently to adhere coating. Place chicken on a wire rack.

Fry chicken in batches, turning occasionally, until a meat thermometer inserted in thickest portion registers 165°, about 12 minutes. Let drain on paper towels. Sprinkle with chives. Drizzle with reserved ½ cup dressing.

5 WAYS WITH
CARAMEL CAKE

CARAMEL CAKE is one of the greatest achievements of the Southern culinary canon. To the guild of Southern grandmothers and those they've taught, stirring together that molten amber mixture is simply second nature. But to the uninitiated, homemade caramel frosting is a method shrouded in mystery.

And perhaps there is some mystique involved. How else can you explain the sudden strength displayed by a grandmother as she takes her wooden spoon to that quickly thickening concoction, whipping it into submission with a fervor that would intimidate any cook half her age?

But in truth, success in caramel only requires two ingredients: knowledge and resolve. With a little know-how, a watchful eye, and a determined spirit, anyone can make a pan-full of sweet and buttery caramel frosting.

Just in case you didn't get a caramel frosting tutorial from your grandmother, we're here to help. Give the recipes on the following pages a good read, then dive right in. When you get it just right, the taste of that smooth, luscious caramel frosting melding into tender yellow cake is reward a-plenty for all your efforts. And you'll make your grandmother proud.

CLASSIC CARAMEL CAKE

This is the cake that all Southerners crave.

──────────── MAKES 1 (9-INCH) CAKE ────────────

CAKE

1 **cup unsalted butter, softened**
2 **cups sugar**
4 **large eggs**
3 **cups all-purpose flour**
1 **tablespoon baking powder**
¾ **teaspoon kosher salt**
1 **cup whole milk**
2 **teaspoons vanilla extract**

FROSTING

1 **cup sour cream**
2 **cups firmly packed dark brown sugar**
1 **cup cold unsalted butter, cubed**
1 **teaspoon kosher salt**
5 **cups confectioners' sugar**
1 **teaspoon vanilla extract**

Preheat oven to 350°. Spray 3 (9-inch) round cake pans with baking spray with flour. Line bottom of pans with parchment paper, and spray pans again.

FOR CAKE In a large bowl, beat butter and sugar with a mixer at medium speed until fluffy, 3 to 4 minutes, stopping to scrape sides of bowl. Add eggs, one at a time, beating well after each addition.

In a medium bowl, whisk together flour, baking powder, and salt. Gradually add flour mixture to butter mixture alternately with milk, beginning and ending with flour mixture, beating just until combined after each addition. Beat in vanilla. Divide batter among prepared pans, smoothing tops. Bake until a wooden pick inserted in center comes out clean, about 22 minutes. Let cool in pans for 10 minutes. Remove from pans, and let cool completely on wire racks.

FOR FROSTING Let sour cream stand at room temperature for 30 minutes. In a large heavy saucepan, bring brown sugar, butter, and salt to a boil over medium heat, stirring constantly. Remove from heat; whisk in sour cream. Bring to a boil over medium heat, stirring constantly. Remove from heat. Gradually add confectioners' sugar and vanilla, beating with a mixer at medium speed until smooth. Let stand at room temperature until mixture begins to thicken, about 20 minutes.

On a cake plate, place 1 cake layer; top with about ¾ cup frosting. Using an offset spatula, gently spread frosting back and forth, leaving a ½-inch border, until frosting thickens. Repeat procedure with second and third cake layers. Secure center of cake with 2 long wooden picks spaced 2 inches apart. Spread a thin layer of frosting around sides of cake; let stand for 20 minutes. Frost top and sides of cake with desired amount of remaining frosting. Remove picks before serving.

CUPCAKES *with* BROWNED BUTTER FROSTING AND CARAMEL SAUCE

These dreamy cupcakes are perfect for your next potluck.

———————————— MAKES ABOUT 28 ————————————

CUPCAKES

1	cup unsalted butter, softened
2	cups sugar
4	large eggs
3	cups all-purpose flour
1	tablespoon baking powder
¾	teaspoon kosher salt
1	cup whole milk
2	teaspoons vanilla extract

FROSTING

1¼	cups unsalted butter, cubed
4	cups confectioners' sugar
¼	cup whole milk
½	teaspoon vanilla extract
¼	teaspoon kosher salt

CARAMEL SAUCE

1	cup sugar
¼	cup water
1	teaspoon light corn syrup
¼	cup cold unsalted butter
½	cup heavy whipping cream
1	teaspoon vanilla extract
½	teaspoon kosher salt

FOR CUPCAKES Preheat oven to 350°. Line 28 muffin cups with paper liners. In a large bowl, beat butter and sugar with a mixer at medium speed until fluffy, 3 to 4 minutes, stopping to scrape sides of bowl. Add eggs, one at a time, beating well after each addition.

In a medium bowl, whisk together flour, baking powder, and salt. Gradually add flour mixture to butter mixture, alternately with milk, beginning and ending with flour mixture, beating just until combined after each addition. Beat in vanilla. Scoop batter into prepared muffin cups, filling about two-thirds full. Bake until a wooden pick inserted in center comes out clean, about 20 minutes. Let cool in pans for 5 minutes. Remove from pans, and let cool completely on a wire rack.

FOR FROSTING In a medium saucepan, melt butter over medium heat. Cook until butter turns medium-brown and has a nutty aroma, about 10 minutes. Pour into a small bowl. Let cool for 10 minutes. Refrigerate until almost firm, about 1 hour, stirring occasionally. In a large bowl, beat browned butter with a mixer at medium speed until creamy. Gradually add confectioners' sugar and milk, beating until smooth. Beat in vanilla and salt. Spread frosting onto cupcakes, making a small well in top of each cupcake. Drizzle about 2 teaspoons Caramel Sauce over each cupcake.

FOR CARAMEL SAUCE In a medium heavy saucepan, sprinkle sugar in an even layer. In a small bowl, stir together ¼ cup water and corn syrup. Pour over sugar, swirling to coat. Cook over medium-high heat, without stirring, until golden brown, about 5 minutes. (While caramel cooks, brush any sugar crystals on sides of pan with a pastry brush dipped in water.) Remove from heat. Add butter, stirring until melted. (Mixture will foam.) In a liquid measuring cup, microwave cream just until hot but not boiling. Pour into caramel, stirring until smooth. Whisk in vanilla and salt. Cover and refrigerate for up to 1 week.

CARAMEL UPSIDE-DOWN CAKE

*This humble cousin of caramel cake makes
its own icing—you can't get easier than that!*

MAKES 1 (10-INCH) CAKE

Caramel Sauce (recipe
   on page 134)
½ cup unsalted butter,
   softened
1   cup sugar
2   large eggs
1½ cups all-purpose flour
1½ teaspoons baking
   powder
½ teaspoon kosher salt
½ cup whole milk
1   teaspoon vanilla
   extract

Preheat oven to 350°. Prepare Caramel Sauce in a 10-inch stainless steel skillet. Set skillet aside.

In a large bowl, beat butter and sugar with a mixer at medium speed until fluffy, 3 to 4 minutes, stopping to scrape sides of bowl. Add eggs, one at a time, beating well after each addition.

In a medium bowl, whisk together flour, baking powder, and salt. Gradually add flour mixture to butter mixture alternately with milk, beginning and ending with flour mixture, beating just until combined after each addition. Beat in vanilla. Drop batter by heaping tablespoonfuls over hot caramel in skillet.

Bake until deep golden brown and a wooden pick inserted in center comes out clean, about 35 minutes. Run a knife around edge of cake to loosen from pan. Immediately place a rimmed plate over cake, and carefully invert. Let cool for 30 minutes.

CARAMEL CAKE TRIFLE

Toasted pecans add crunch to the layers of buttery cake, sweet caramel, and whipped cream.

SERVES ABOUT 10

Caramel Sauce (recipe on page 134)

CAKE
- ½ cup unsalted butter, softened
- 1 cup sugar
- 2 large eggs
- 1½ cups all-purpose flour
- 1½ teaspoons baking powder
- ½ teaspoon kosher salt
- ½ cup whole milk
- 1 teaspoon vanilla extract

WHIPPED CREAM
- 3½ cups heavy whipping cream
- ⅔ cup sour cream
- ⅔ cup confectioners' sugar
- 1 teaspoon vanilla extract

- 1 cup chopped toasted pecans, divided
- Garnish: chopped toasted pecans

Prepare Caramel Sauce in a 10-inch stainless steel skillet. Set skillet aside.

Preheat oven to 350°. Spray a deep 9-inch round cake pan with baking spray with flour. Line bottom of pan with parchment paper, and spray pan again.

FOR CAKE In a large bowl, beat butter and sugar with a mixer at medium speed until fluffy, 3 to 4 minutes, stopping to scrape sides of bowl. Add eggs, one at a time, beating well after each addition.

In a medium bowl, whisk together flour, baking powder, and salt. Gradually add flour mixture to butter mixture alternately with milk, beginning and ending with flour mixture, beating just until combined after each addition. Beat in vanilla. Spread into prepared pan. Bake until a wooden pick inserted in center comes out clean, about 30 minutes. Let cool in pan for 10 minutes. Remove from pan, and let cool completely on a wire rack.

FOR WHIPPED CREAM In a large bowl, beat cream, sour cream, confectioners' sugar, and vanilla with a mixer at high speed until soft peaks form.

Cut cake into 1-inch cubes. In a large trifle dish, place one-third of cake cubes. Spread 2½ cups whipped cream over cake. Drizzle 1 cup caramel over whipped cream. Sprinkle with ½ cup pecans. Repeat layers once. Top with remaining cake and remaining whipped cream. Drizzle with remaining caramel. Garnish with pecans, if desired. Cover and refrigerate for 30 minutes before serving.

5

EASY CARAMEL SHEET CAKE

Never made a caramel cake? This one-layer version is simple to frost.

— SERVES 12 —

CAKE

1	cup unsalted butter
1½	cups sugar
4	large eggs, separated
3	cups cake flour
1	teaspoon baking powder
1	teaspoon baking soda
½	teaspoon salt
1¼	cups coconut milk
1	teaspoon vanilla extract

FROSTING

3	cups confectioners' sugar, sifted
¾	cup unsalted butter, softened
1½	cups firmly packed dark brown sugar
5	tablespoons whole milk
1½	teaspoons vanilla extract
½	teaspoon salt

Garnish: chopped toasted pecans
Caramel Sauce (recipe on page 134)

FOR CAKE Preheat oven to 350°. Spray a 13x9-inch baking dish with baking spray with flour. In a large bowl, beat butter and sugar with a mixer at medium speed until fluffy, 3 to 4 minutes, stopping to scrape sides of bowl. Add egg yolks, one at a time, beating well after each addition.

In a medium bowl, whisk together flour, baking powder, baking soda, and salt. With mixer on low speed, gradually add flour mixture to butter mixture alternately with coconut milk, beginning and ending with flour mixture, beating just until combined after each addition. Beat in vanilla.

In a medium bowl, using clean beaters, beat egg whites with a mixer at high speed just until stiff peaks form. (Do not overbeat.) Gently fold egg whites into batter. Gently spread batter into prepared pan.

Bake until a wooden pick inserted in center comes out clean, 25 to 30 minutes. Let cool completely on a wire rack.

FOR FROSTING In a large bowl, place confectioners' sugar. Set aside. In a medium heavy saucepan, place butter. Cook over medium heat until butter is melted; stir in brown sugar. Bring to a simmer, and cook for 1 minute, stirring constantly. Remove from heat; stir in milk.

Return to heat; bring mixture to a simmer, and cook for 1 minute, stirring constantly. Pour into confectioners' sugar. Add vanilla and salt; beat with a mixer at medium speed until smooth. Pour over cake, spreading back and forth with an offset spatula until frosting begins to thicken. Garnish with pecans, if desired. Drizzle with Caramel Sauce.

5 WAYS WITH

PECAN PIE

THERE'S SOMETHING about a home-baked, hot-from-the-oven pie that leaves the other desserts in the dust. And while the South is known for quite a few varieties, the reigning king of these sliceable sweets is undeniably the pecan pie. With its flaky crust and gooey filling, there's a reason this dessert is an icon. It's composed of an addictive combination of butter, eggs, sugar, and vanilla, poured over a generous pile of pecans, all nestled in a piecrust and baked until your kitchen is filled with its rich, buttery aroma.

The hardest part of the process? Waiting until this caramelized beauty is cool enough to cut into. And sometimes, you can't wait—and that's OK. So what if your slice is more of scoop, one that causes your ice cream to melt on contact?

But if you do exercise just a bit more restraint and let your pie fully cool, each slice becomes a glorious cross section of amber-hued layers that needs no extra decoration. And while it's most often dished up during the cooler months, there's no wrong time of year to indulge in a slice of pecan pie.

1

CLASSIC PECAN PIE

*A Southern staple, this treasured pie
is the perfect dessert for any time of year.*

CRUST
- 1¼ cups all-purpose flour
- 1 teaspoon kosher salt
- 1 teaspoon sugar
- ½ cup cold unsalted butter, cubed
- 3 to 4 tablespoons whole buttermilk, chilled

FILLING
- 3 large eggs
- 1 cup firmly packed light brown sugar
- ¾ cup light corn syrup
- ½ cup unsalted butter, melted and cooled to room temperature
- 1 teaspoon vanilla extract
- 1 teaspoon kosher salt
- 2 cups pecan halves

FOR CRUST Preheat oven to 350°. In a medium bowl, stir together flour, salt, and sugar. Using a pastry blender or 2 forks, cut in cold butter until mixture is crumbly.

Add buttermilk, 1 tablespoon at a time, stirring until a dough forms. Shape dough into a disk, and wrap tightly in plastic wrap. Refrigerate for at least 30 minutes.

On a lightly floured surface, roll dough ⅛-inch thick. Transfer to a 9-inch pie plate, pressing into bottom and up sides. Fold edges under, and crimp as desired.

FOR FILLING In a medium bowl, stir together eggs, brown sugar, corn syrup, melted butter, vanilla, and salt. Gently stir in pecans. Pour mixture into prepared crust.

Bake for 30 minutes. Loosely cover with foil, and bake until center is set, about 20 minutes more. Let cool completely on a wire rack.

PECAN PIE THUMBPRINT COOKIES

Buttery and packed with pecans, these one-bite cookies are a delight.

———————— MAKES 60 ————————

4   **cups pecan halves**
2   **teaspoons kosher salt, divided**
1   **teaspoon grated fresh nutmeg, divided**
2   **cups unsalted butter, softened**
1⅓ **cups sugar**
4   **large egg yolks**
2   **teaspoons vanilla extract**
4   **cups all-purpose flour**
Pecan Pie Filling, slightly warmed (recipe follows)

PECAN PIE FILLING
¾   **cup chopped pecans**
½   **cup sugar**
⅓   **cup dark corn syrup**
2½ **tablespoons unsalted butter, melted**
1   **large egg**
½   **teaspoon vanilla extract**
⅛   **teaspoon kosher salt**

In the work bowl of a food processor, combine pecans, 1 teaspoon salt, and ½ teaspoon nutmeg. Pulse until nuts are finely ground. Transfer mixture to a medium bowl.

In a large bowl, beat butter and sugar with a mixer at medium speed until creamy, 3 to 4 minutes, stopping to scrape sides of bowl. Add egg yolks, one at a time, beating well after each addition. Beat in vanilla. With mixer on low speed, add flour, ½ cup chopped nut mixture, remaining 1 teaspoon salt, and remaining ½ teaspoon nutmeg. Increase mixer speed to medium, and beat just until mixture comes together, about 2 minutes. Cover and refrigerate for 1 hour.

Preheat oven to 350°. Line several baking sheets with parchment paper. Using floured hands, roll dough into 60 (1-inch) balls. Roll balls in remaining nut mixture. Place 2 inches apart on prepared pans. Using your thumb or the back of a spoon, gently make an indentation in center of each ball.

Bake for 10 minutes; remove from oven, and press down centers again. Bake until edges are lightly browned, about 4 minutes more. Let cool on pans for 2 minutes. Remove from pans, and let cool completely on wire racks. Spoon 1 teaspoon Pecan Pie Filling in center of each cookie. Let stand until filling cools.

FOR PECAN PIE FILLING In a medium saucepan, bring pecans, sugar, corn syrup, melted butter, egg, vanilla, and salt to a boil over medium-high heat, stirring frequently. Reduce heat to medium-low; simmer, stirring constantly, until thickened, 3 to 4 minutes. Let cool to room temperature before using.

3

PECAN PIE CAKE

This cake's deliciously gooey filling will please any pecan pie fan.

———————— MAKES 1 (9-INCH) CAKE ————————

1 cup toasted pecans, chopped
1½ cups unsalted butter, softened
2½ cups firmly packed dark brown sugar
4 large eggs
3 cups all-purpose flour
2 teaspoons baking powder
1 teaspoon kosher salt
1¼ cups whole milk
1 tablespoon vanilla extract
Pecan Pie Filling (recipe on page 146)
Brown Sugar Frosting (recipe follows)
Garnish: toasted chopped pecans

BROWN SUGAR FROSTING
1 cup firmly packed dark brown sugar
⅓ cup water
½ teaspoon kosher salt
2 cups unsalted butter, softened and divided
7½ cups confectioners' sugar
1 to 3 tablespoons whole milk

Preheat oven to 350°. Spray 2 (9-inch) deep round cake pans with baking spray with flour. Line bottom of pans with parchment paper, and spray pans again.

Sprinkle ½ cup chopped pecans in each prepared pan. In a large bowl, beat butter and brown sugar with a mixer at medium speed until fluffy, 3 to 4 minutes, stopping to scrape sides of bowl. Add eggs, one at a time, beating well after each addition.

In a medium bowl, whisk together flour, baking powder, and salt. With mixer on low speed, gradually add flour mixture to butter mixture, alternately with milk, beginning and ending with flour mixture, beating just until combined after each addition. Beat in vanilla. Pour batter over pecans in prepared pans, smoothing tops.

Bake until a wooden pick inserted in center comes out clean, about 30 minutes. Let cool in pans for 10 minutes. Remove from pans, and let cool completely on wire racks. Spread Pecan Pie Filling between layers. Spread Brown Sugar Frosting on top and sides of cake. Garnish with pecans, if desired.

FOR BROWN SUGAR FROSTING In a small saucepan, bring brown sugar, ⅓ cup water, and salt to a boil over medium-high heat. Cook, stirring constantly, until sugar is dissolved, about 2 minutes. Remove from heat; stir in ½ cup butter. Let cool completely.

In a large bowl, beat cooled brown sugar mixture and remaining 1½ cups butter with a mixer at medium speed until creamy. With mixer on low speed, gradually add confectioners' sugar, beating until combined. Add milk, 1 tablespoon at a time, until frosting reaches a spreadable consistency.

BROWNED BUTTER PECAN TASSIES

Nutty and rich, browned butter takes these tassies to the next level.

───────────── **MAKES ABOUT 24** ─────────────

DOUGH

½   **cup browned butter, softened (see note)**

4   **ounces cream cheese, softened**

1¼ **cups all-purpose flour**

1   **tablespoon sugar**

¾   **teaspoon salt**

FILLING

½   **cup firmly packed light brown sugar**

1   **tablespoon browned butter, melted**

1   **tablespoon corn syrup**

1   **tablespoon cane syrup**

1   **teaspoon vanilla extract**

⅛   **teaspoon salt**

1   **large egg, lightly beaten**

⅔   **cup chopped pecans**

24 **pecan halves**

FOR DOUGH In a large bowl, beat softened browned butter and cream cheese with a mixer at medium speed until smooth. Gradually add flour, sugar, and salt; beat at low speed until a firm dough forms, stopping to scrape sides of bowl. Turn out dough onto a lightly floured surface, and shape into a disk. Wrap in plastic wrap, and refrigerate for 30 minutes.

Preheat oven to 350°. Spray 24 miniature muffin cups with baking spray with flour. Scoop 24 heaping tablespoonfuls of dough. Using your hands, roll into balls. Place 1 ball in each prepared muffin cup, pressing into bottom and up sides.

FOR FILLING In a small bowl, whisk together brown sugar, melted browned butter, corn syrup, cane syrup, vanilla, salt, and egg.

Sprinkle ½ teaspoon chopped pecans in each muffin cup. Spoon 1½ teaspoons syrup mixture over pecans. Top with pecan halves.

Bake until set and lightly browned, about 20 minutes. Let cool in pans for 5 minutes. Run a knife around edges to loosen; gently remove from muffin cups. Let cool completely on a wire rack. Store in an airtight container for up to 3 days.

NOTE: *To make browned butter, heat ¾ cup unsalted butter in a medium, stainless-steel skillet over medium heat until butter is golden brown and has a nutty aroma, 7 to 8 minutes. Strain through a fine-mesh sieve into a small bowl. Cover and refrigerate for 45 minutes, stirring twice.*

5

PECAN SLAB PIE

Feeding a crowd? This is the pecan pie for you.

———— MAKES ABOUT 16 SERVINGS ————

CRUST
2½ cups all-purpose flour
2 teaspoons sugar
2 teaspoons kosher salt
1 cup cold unsalted
 butter, cubed
½ cup whole buttermilk

FILLING
6 cups pecan halves
6 large eggs
1¾ cups firmly packed
 light brown sugar
1½ cups light corn syrup
¾ cup unsalted butter,
 melted
2 tablespoons
 all-purpose flour
2 teaspoons kosher salt
2 teaspoons vanilla
 extract
1 teaspoon orange zest

FOR CRUST In a medium bowl, whisk together flour, sugar, and salt. Using a pastry blender or 2 forks, cut in cold butter until mixture is crumbly. Gradually add buttermilk, stirring with a fork just until dry ingredients are moistened. Turn out dough, and shape into a disk. Wrap in plastic wrap, and refrigerate for at least 1 hour.

Preheat oven to 350°. Let dough stand at room temperature until slightly softened, about 20 minutes.

On a lightly floured surface, roll dough into a 17½x12½-inch rectangle. Transfer to a 15¼x10¼-inch jelly-roll pan, pressing into bottom and up sides. Fold edges under, and crimp as desired. Top with a piece of parchment paper, letting ends extend over edges of pan. Add pie weights.

Bake for 20 minutes. Carefully remove paper and weights. Reduce oven to 325°.

FOR FILLING Sprinkle pecans in prepared crust. In a large bowl, whisk eggs until foamy. Whisk in brown sugar, corn syrup, melted butter, flour, salt, vanilla, and zest until well combined. Pour over pecans.

Bake until crust is golden brown and filling is set, about 40 minutes, loosely covering with foil to prevent excess browning, if necessary. Let cool completely on a wire rack.

5 WAYS WITH
STARTERS & STAPLES

SOUTHERNERS ARE SOCIAL PEOPLE. Morning, noon, or night, they love to stop by for a visit. But no social gathering in the South is complete without just a little something to nibble on. Hence this little "lagniappe" of tasty recipes for snacks, starters, and staples.

When company's on the way, there's nothing easier to make than a batch of homemade pimiento cheese. Served with your favorite crackers and pickles, this simple snack is always a hit. A little higher on the effort scale are those beloved Southern staples, cheese straws, and deviled eggs. Sure, they take a little planning, but the delicious results are worth the extra work.

And because you never know when a neighbor's going to come knocking at your door, there's a handful of biscuit recipes for you. It's one Southern delight that hits the spot, day or night.

5 WAYS WITH

DEVILED EGGS

No self-respecting Southerner can turn down a deviled egg.

— MAKES 24 —

12	large hard-cooked eggs, peeled and halved lengthwise
½	cup mayonnaise*
1	teaspoon fresh lemon juice
1	teaspoon Dijon mustard
¼	teaspoon kosher salt

We used Duke's Mayonnaise.

In a medium bowl, mash egg yolks with a fork. Stir in mayonnaise, lemon juice, mustard, and salt until smooth.

Spoon filling into egg whites. Garnish with desired toppings. Refrigerate until ready to serve.

2 BARBECUE

Top Deviled Eggs with **barbecue seasoning, shredded Cheddar cheese, chopped dill pickles**, and **barbecue sauce**.

1 SPICED PECAN + SWEET ONIONS

Top Deviled Eggs with **sautéed sweet onions** and **Spiced Pecans** (recipe follows)

4 MISSISSIPPI STYLE

Top Deviled Eggs with **Comeback Sauce** (recipe below) and **crumbled toasted saltine crackers**.

3 HOT & SPICY

Top Deviled Eggs with **fried chicken skin** and **hot sauce**.

SPICED PECANS

Makes about 3 cups

1	**large egg white**
1	**tablespoon water**
3	**cups pecan halves**
1	**teaspoon salt**
1	**teaspoon sugar**
½	**teaspoon ground red pepper**
¼	**teaspoon ground black pepper**

Preheat oven to 350°. Line a baking sheet with foil. In a medium bowl, beat egg white and 1 tablespoon water until frothy. Stir in pecans until combined. Using a slotted spoon, transfer pecans to prepared pan; spread in a single layer. Discard any remaining egg white mixture.

In a small bowl, stir together salt, sugar, red pepper, and black pepper. Sprinkle over pecans. Bake, stirring occasionally, until almost dry, about 30 minutes. Let cool completely.

5 BACON RANCH

Prepare Deviled Eggs, omitting salt. Stir **1½ teaspoons ranch dressing mix** into egg yolk mixture. Top with **chopped cooked bacon** and **chopped fresh herbs**.

COMEBACK SAUCE

Makes about 1½ cups

1	**cup mayonnaise**
¼	**cup chili sauce**
½	**teaspoon garlic salt**
½	**teaspoon ground black pepper**
½	**teaspoon Worcestershire sauce**
¼	**teaspoon onion powder**

In a medium bowl, whisk together all ingredients. Cover and refrigerate for up to 1 week.

5 WAYS *WITH*

CHEESE STRAWS

With this classic recipe, you can turn out ethereal cheese straws worthy of a Southern grandmother.

———————— MAKES ABOUT 48 ————————

1 CHEESE STRAWS

2   cups all-purpose flour
2   cups shredded sharp Cheddar cheese
¾   cup cold unsalted butter, cubed
1   teaspoon kosher salt
¼   teaspoon ground black pepper
¼   teaspoon ground red pepper
¼   teaspoon smoked paprika
¼   cup plus 1 tablespoon whole milk

Preheat oven to 350°. Line 2 baking sheets with parchment paper. In the work bowl of a food processor, place flour, cheese, butter, salt, black pepper, red pepper, and paprika; pulse to combine. With processor running, add milk in a slow, steady stream until mixture forms a dough.

Using a cookie press fitted with a star-shaped disk, pipe dough into long straight lines on prepared pans; cut into 4-inch pieces. Bake until lightly browned, 18 to 20 minutes. Let cool completely on pans. Store in an airtight container for up to 5 days.

2 CHEESE COINS

Roll dough into a log. Wrap in plastic wrap, and freeze until firm, about 20 minutes. Unwrap dough, and cut into ¼-inch-thick slices. Bake until crisp, about 18 minutes.

3 CHEESE STICKS

Roll pieces of dough into thin 6-inch logs. Bake until crisp, 18 to 20 minutes. Garnish with paprika, if desired.

ROASTED SHALLOT TART WITH CHEESE STRAW CRUST

MAKES 1 (9-INCH) TART

CRUST

1	cup all-purpose flour
1	cup shredded sharp Cheddar cheese
10	tablespoons cold unsalted butter, cubed
¾	teaspoon kosher salt
⅛	teaspoon ground black pepper
⅛	teaspoon ground red pepper
⅛	teaspoon smoked paprika
2	tablespoons whole milk

SHALLOTS

8	shallots, halved
1	tablespoon extra-virgin olive oil
1	teaspoon kosher salt
¼	teaspoon ground black pepper

CUSTARD

1	large egg
¾	cup heavy whipping cream
¼	teaspoon kosher salt
⅛	teaspoon ground black pepper

1	tablespoon fresh thyme leaves

Preheat oven to 350°. Spray a 9-inch square, removable-bottom tart pan with cooking spray. Line a baking sheet with parchment paper.

FOR CRUST In the work bowl of a food processor, place flour, cheese, butter, salt, black pepper, red pepper, and paprika; pulse to combine. With processor running, add milk in a slow, steady stream until mixture forms a dough.

On a lightly floured surface, roll dough into a ¼-inch-thick square. Transfer to prepared tart pan, pressing into bottom and up sides. Trim excess dough. Top with a piece of parchment paper, letting ends extend over edges of pan. Add pie weights. Bake for 15 minutes. Carefully remove paper and weights. Bake until golden brown, 10 to 15 minutes more. Let cool on a wire rack. Increase oven temperature to 425°.

FOR SHALLOTS Place shallots on prepared baking sheet. Drizzle with oil, and sprinkle with salt and pepper. Bake until shallots are golden brown and caramelized, about 25 minutes. Reduce oven temperature to 350°.

FOR CUSTARD In a small bowl, whisk together egg, cream, salt, and pepper. Pour mixture into cooled crust; top with shallots, and sprinkle with thyme. Bake until custard is set, about 15 minutes. Serve warm or at room temperature.

BLUE CHEESE COINS WITH RASPBERRY PRESERVES

MAKES 30 SANDWICH COOKIES

2	cups all-purpose flour
2	cups crumbled blue cheese
¾	cup cold unsalted butter, cubed
1	teaspoon kosher salt
¼	teaspoon ground black pepper
¼	cup whole milk

Seedless raspberry preserves

In the work bowl of a food processor, place flour, cheese, butter, salt, and pepper; pulse to combine. With processor running, add milk in a slow, steady stream until mixture forms a dough.

Divide dough in half, and roll each half into a log. Wrap in parchment paper, and freeze until firm, about 2 hours.

Preheat oven to 350°. Line 2 baking sheets with parchment paper.

Slice dough into ⅛-inch-thick rounds, and place 1 inch apart on prepared pans. Bake until golden brown around the edges, 18 to 20 minutes. Let cool completely on wire racks. Spoon about 1 teaspoon preserves onto flat side of half of coins. Place remaining coins, flat side down, on top of preserves. Store unfilled coins in an airtight container for up to 5 days.

5 WAYS WITH

PICKLES

When nature blesses you with an abundance of vegetables, it's time to make refrigerator pickles.

— MAKES 2 (1-QUART) JARS —

1 REFRIGERATOR PICKLES

3	cups water
1½	cups apple cider vinegar
¼	cup kosher salt
1	tablespoon chopped fresh garlic
1	tablespoon yellow mustard seed
1	tablespoon dill seed
2	teaspoons sugar
1	teaspoon black peppercorns
2	pounds small cucumbers, ends trimmed, sliced as desired (see note)
4	sprigs fresh dill

In a medium saucepan, bring 3 cups water, vinegar, salt, garlic, mustard seed, dill seed, sugar, and peppercorns to a boil over medium-high heat. Remove from heat, and let cool to room temperature.

Divide cucumber and dill sprigs between 2 (1-quart) jars; add cooled vinegar mixture to cover. Seal jars; refrigerate for at least 24 hours or up to 1 month.

NOTE: *Slice the cucumbers into your preferred pickle shape—halves, quarters, or chips.*

2 DILLY BEANS
MAKES 5 (1-PINT) JARS

- 3 cups distilled white vinegar
- 3 cups water
- 5 cloves garlic, smashed
- ¼ cup pickling salt
- 1 tablespoon sugar
- 1 teaspoon black peppercorns
- 2½ teaspoons dill seed
- 2½ teaspoons yellow mustard seed
- 1¼ teaspoons crushed red pepper
- 1 large carrot, peeled and cut into 5 sticks
- 10 sprigs fresh dill
- 2½ pounds French green beans, blanched

In a medium saucepan, bring vinegar, 3 cups water, garlic, salt, and sugar to a boil over medium-high heat. Remove from heat; let cool to room temperature. Discard garlic. In each of 5 (1-pint) jars, place about 10 peppercorns, ½ teaspoon dill seed, ½ teaspoon mustard seed, ¼ teaspoon red pepper, 1 carrot stick, and 2 dill sprigs. Divide beans among jars; add vinegar mixture to cover. Seal jars; refrigerate for at least 48 hours or up to 1 month.

3 PICKLED SWEET PEPPERS
MAKES 2 (1-PINT) JARS

- 1 pound small sweet peppers, thinly sliced (about 4 cups)
- 3 large shallots, sliced into rings
- 1½ cups white wine vinegar
- ½ cup water
- 2 cloves garlic, smashed
- ¼ cup plus 1 tablespoon sugar
- 1 tablespoon plus 1 teaspoon kosher salt
- ½ teaspoon crushed red pepper

Divide peppers and shallots between 2 (1-pint) jars. In a medium saucepan, bring vinegar, ½ cup water, garlic, sugar, salt, and red pepper to a boil over medium-high heat. Remove from heat; discard garlic. Divide vinegar mixture between jars. Seal jars, and let cool to room temperature. Refrigerate for at least 24 hours or up to 1 month.

4 WATERMELON RIND PICKLES

MAKES 2 (1-PINT) JARS

- 1 **cup sugar**
- 1 **cup water**
- 1 **cup Champagne vinegar (see Note)**
- 1 **lemon, sliced**
- 2 **teaspoons yellow mustard seed**
- 1½ **teaspoons crushed red pepper**
- 1½ **teaspoons kosher salt**
- 1 **teaspoon black peppercorns**
- 2 **whole star anise**
- 1 **stick cinnamon**
- 4 **cups cubed peeled watermelon rind**

In a medium saucepan, bring sugar, 1 cup water, vinegar, lemon, mustard seed, red pepper, salt, peppercorns, star anise, and cinnamon to a boil over medium-high heat. Reduce heat to medium-low. Add watermelon rind; simmer until tender, about 10 minutes. Remove from heat; let cool in pan for 5 minutes. Discard lemon and cinnamon.

Divide watermelon rind between 2 (1-pint) jars; add vinegar mixture to cover. Seal jars, and let cool to room temperature. Refrigerate for at least 3 hours or up to 1 month.

NOTE: *Don't have Champagne vinegar? Substitute white wine vinegar.*

5 PICKLED SWEET CORN

MAKES 3 (1-PINT) JARS

8	ears fresh yellow corn, shucked
⅓	cup chopped shallot
3	small red chile peppers, thinly sliced, such as Fresno
9	black peppercorns
¾	teaspoon cumin seed
2	cups apple cider vinegar
½	cup dry white wine
½	cup water
3	cloves garlic, smashed
3	tablespoons kosher salt
1	teaspoon sugar

Cut corn kernels from cobs; discard cobs. In a medium bowl, combine corn kernels, shallot, peppers, peppercorns, and cumin seed. Divide corn mixture among 3 (1-pint) jars.

In a medium saucepan, bring vinegar, wine, ½ cup water, garlic, salt, and sugar to a boil over medium-high heat. Remove from heat; discard garlic.

Divide vinegar mixture among jars. Seal jars, and let cool to room temperature. Refrigerate for at least 24 hours or up to 1 month.

5 WAYS *WITH*

PIMIENTO CHEESE

This classic version is great on grilled cheese sandwiches, crackers, or served with crispy vegetables.

—————— MAKES ABOUT 3 CUPS ——————

1 CLASSIC PIMIENTO CHEESE

2   cups shredded mild Cheddar cheese
1   (8-ounce) package cream cheese, softened
1   (4-ounce) jar diced pimientos, drained
½   cup mayonnaise
½   teaspoon kosher salt
¼   teaspoon garlic powder
¼   teaspoon onion powder
¼   teaspoon ground red pepper
Grilled bread and pickles, to serve

In a medium bowl, stir together Cheddar, cream cheese, pimientos, mayonnaise, salt, garlic powder, onion powder, and red pepper until well combined. Serve with crackers and pickles, if desired.

2 JALAPEÑO-BACON PIMIENTO CHEESE

In a large bowl, stir together **Classic Pimiento Cheese**, **6 slices bacon, cooked and crumbled**, and **1 jalapeño pepper, seeded and diced** until combined. Garnish with bacon, if desired.

3 SMOKED PIMIENTO CHEESE

In a large bowl, stir together **Classic Pimiento Cheese**, replacing half of Cheddar cheese with **8 ounces of shredded smoked Cheddar cheese**. Stir in **¼ teaspoon smoked paprika**.

4 HERBED PIMIENTO CHEESE

Prepare **Classic Pimiento Cheese**, reducing salt to ¼ teaspoon. Add **¼ cup chopped green onion**, **3 tablespoons capers**, **2 teaspoons chopped fresh dill** , and **⅛ teaspoon lemon zest**, stirring until combined. Garnish with green onion, capers, and dill, if desired.

5 ROASTED GARLIC-CHIPOTLE PIMIENTO CHEESE

Cut ½ inch off a head of garlic, and drizzle with **1 teaspoon olive oil**. Wrap in foil, and roast in a 400° oven for 30 minutes. Let cool, and remove roasted garlic cloves. Stir into **Classic Pimiento Cheese** along with **2 teaspoons puréed chipotle peppers in adobo sauce**.

5 WAYS WITH

FRIED VEGETABLES

Encased in crispy breading, these fried vegetables are the tops.

SERVES 8

1

GREEN TOMATOES

2

ZUCCHINI

3

PICKLED OKRA

3   medium green tomatoes,
    cut into ¼-inch-thick slices
2   medium zucchini, cut into
    ¼-inch-thick slices
5   teaspoons kosher salt, divided
2⅔ cups plain yellow stone-ground
    cornmeal
1⅓ cups panko (Japanese bread
    crumbs)
1⅓ cups all-purpose flour
1½ teaspoons ground black pepper
2   cups whole buttermilk
Vegetable oil, for frying
1   (16-ounce) jar whole pickled
    okra, drained and patted dry
Hot sauce, to serve

Place tomato and zucchini slices on several layers of paper towels. Sprinkle both sides with 2 teaspoons salt. Let stand for 30 minutes. Pat dry with paper towels. In a shallow dish, whisk together cornmeal, bread crumbs, flour, pepper, and remaining 3 teaspoons salt. In another shallow dish, place buttermilk.

In a large Dutch oven, pour oil to fill halfway, and heat over medium heat until a deep-fry thermometer registers 350°.

Dip tomato slices in buttermilk, letting excess drip off. Dredge in cornmeal mixture, shaking off excess. Working in batches, carefully place tomato slices in hot oil. Fry, turning occasionally, until golden brown, 2 to 3 minutes. Remove using a slotted spoon, and let drain on a wire rack. Repeat with zucchini and okra. Sprinkle with additional salt and pepper. Serve with hot sauce.

4 FRIED OKRA
SERVES 4 TO 6

½ cup whole milk
1 large egg
1¼ cups all-purpose flour
⅔ cup plain white or yellow cornmeal
2 tablespoons cornstarch
1 teaspoon kosher salt, divided
½ teaspoon garlic powder
¼ teaspoon ground black pepper
Vegetable oil for frying
½ pound small to medium fresh okra, halved lengthwise
Hot sauce (optional)

In a shallow dish, whisk together milk and egg. In another shallow dish, whisk together flour, cornmeal, cornstarch, ½ teaspoon salt, garlic powder, and pepper.

In a large deep skillet, fill with oil to halfway full. Heat over medium-high heat until a deep-fry thermometer reads 350°. Dip okra in egg mixture, allowing excess to drip off. Dredge in cornmeal mixture, shaking off excess.

Gently add okra to hot oil. Cook in batches until golden brown, about 3 minutes, turning occasionally. (Adjust heat as needed to maintain 350°.) Remove okra from skillet, and let drain on paper towels.

Sprinkle okra with remaining ½ teaspoon salt. Serve with hot sauce, if desired.

5 FRIED JALAPEÑOS
SERVES 4 TO 6

½ cup whole milk
1 large egg
1¼ cups all-purpose flour
⅔ cup plain white or yellow cornmeal
2 tablespoons cornstarch
1 teaspoon kosher salt, divided
½ teaspoon garlic powder
¼ teaspoon ground black pepper
Vegetable oil for frying
2 (12-ounce) jars whole pickled jalapeños, drained and halved lengthwise
Hot sauce (optional)

In a shallow dish, whisk together milk and egg. In another shallow dish, whisk together flour, cornmeal, cornstarch, ½ teaspoon salt, garlic powder, and pepper.

In a large deep skillet, fill with oil to halfway full. Heat over medium-high heat until a deep-fry thermometer reads 350°. Dip jalapeños in egg mixture, allowing excess to drip off. Dredge in cornmeal mixture, shaking off excess.

Gently add jalapeños to hot oil. Cook in batches until golden brown, about 3 minutes, turning occasionally. (Adjust heat as needed to maintain 350°.) Remove jalapeños from skillet, and let drain on paper towels.

Sprinkle jalapeños with remaining ½ teaspoon salt. Serve with hot sauce, if desired.

5 WAYS *WITH*

BISCUITS

These biscuits are so easy to make, you'll want to serve them at every meal.

---

1 BUTTERMILK BISCUITS
MAKES 10

2½ cups self-rising flour
2 tablespoons sugar
½ cup cold unsalted butter, cubed
¾ cup cold whole buttermilk
2 tablespoons unsalted butter, melted

Preheat oven to 425°. Line a baking sheet with parchment paper.

In a large bowl, stir together flour and sugar. Using a pastry blender or 2 forks, cut in cold butter until mixture is crumbly. Stir in buttermilk just until combined.

Turn out dough onto a heavily floured surface. Fold dough in half until it comes together, 3 or 4 times. Pat or roll dough to 1-inch thickness. Using a 2½-inch round cutter dipped in flour, cut dough without twisting cutter, rerolling scraps as necessary.

Place biscuits 2 inches apart on prepared pan. Freeze until cold, about 10 minutes. Brush with melted butter. Bake until golden brown, about 12 minutes.

2 BACON-CHEDDAR BISCUITS
MAKES 16

2½ cups self-rising flour
1 tablespoon sugar
1 teaspoon ground black pepper
½ cup cold bacon drippings
2 tablespoons cold unsalted butter, cubed
1 cup shredded sharp yellow Cheddar cheese
½ cup crumbled cooked bacon
¾ cup cold whole buttermilk
2 tablespoons unsalted butter, melted

Preheat oven to 425°. Line a baking sheet with parchment paper. In a large bowl, stir together flour, sugar, and pepper. Using a pastry blender or 2 forks, cut in bacon drippings and cold butter until mixture is crumbly. Stir in cheese, cooked bacon, and buttermilk just until combined.

Turn out dough onto a heavily floured surface. Fold dough in half until it comes together, 3 to 4 times. Pat or roll dough to 1-inch thickness. Using a knife dipped in flour, cut dough into 2-inch squares. Place biscuits 2 inches apart on prepared pan. Freeze until cold, about 10 minutes. Brush with melted butter. Bake until golden brown, about 12 minutes.

3 PECAN AND GOAT CHEESE BISCUITS MAKES 16

4   cups self-rising flour
1   teaspoon kosher salt
¾   cup cold unsalted butter, cubed
1½ cups pecans, chopped
6   ounces crumbled goat cheese, chilled
2   teaspoons fresh thyme, roughly chopped
1¾ cups whole buttermilk
2   tablespoons unsalted butter, melted
Garnish: cane syrup

Preheat oven to 425°. Spray a 12-inch cast-iron skillet with cooking spray. In a large bowl, sift together flour and salt. Using a pastry blender or 2 forks, cut in cold butter until mixture is crumbly. Stir in pecans, goat cheese, and thyme. Add buttermilk, and toss with your hands until a sticky dough forms. Using a ¼-cup scoop, drop biscuits into prepared skillet. Brush with melted butter.

Bake until tops are golden, 30 to 35 minutes, loosely covering with foil to prevent excess browning, if necessary. Garnish with cane syrup, if desired.

4 SWEET POTATO BISCUITS MAKES 12

2   cups all-purpose flour
2   tablespoons sugar
1   tablespoon baking powder
¾   teaspoon kosher salt
¼   teaspoon ground ginger
¼   teaspoon ground nutmeg
½   cup cold unsalted butter, cubed
⅓   cup toasted pecans, chopped
1   (15-ounce) can cut sweet potatoes in
     syrup, drained well and coarsely mashed
¾   cup whole buttermilk, divided
1   tablespoon unsalted butter, melted

Preheat oven to 425°. In a large bowl, whisk together flour, sugar, baking powder, salt, ginger, and nutmeg. Using a pastry blender or 2 forks, cut in cold butter until mixture is crumbly. Add pecans, sweet potatoes, and ⅔ cup buttermilk, tossing until ingredients are moistened. Add remaining buttermilk, if needed. (Dough will be sticky.)

On a heavily floured surface, gently knead dough 4 or 5 times. Roll dough to ¾-inch thickness. Fold dough in half; roll to ¾-inch thickness. Using a 2½-inch round cutter dipped in flour, cut dough, rerolling scraps once. Place biscuits on a 12-inch cast-iron griddle or skillet. Bake until lightly browned, about 17 minutes. Brush with melted butter.

5 WHITE CHEDDAR–CHIVE DROP BISCUITS MAKES 18

2½ cups all-purpose flour
1   tablespoon sugar
2   teaspoons baking powder
½   teaspoon baking soda
½   teaspoon kosher salt
6   tablespoons cold unsalted butter, cubed
2   cups shredded white Cheddar cheese
3   tablespoons chopped fresh chives
1½ cups whole buttermilk

Preheat oven to 400°. Line a large baking sheet with parchment paper. In a large bowl, whisk together flour, sugar, baking powder, baking soda, and salt. Using a pastry blender or 2 forks, cut in cold butter until mixture is crumbly. Add cheese and chives, tossing with a fork.

Make a well in center of flour mixture. Add buttermilk, tossing with a fork until a sticky dough forms. Drop dough by ¼ cupfuls 2 inches apart onto prepared pan. Bake until lightly browned, 16 to 18 minutes. Let cool on pan for 2 minutes. Remove from pan, and let cool completely on a wire rack.

RECIPE INDEX